Tobacco

DRUGS OF ABUSE
A Comprehensive Series for Clinicians

A Continuation Order Plan is available for this series. A continuation order will bring delivery of each new volume immediately upon publication. Volumes are billed only upon actual shipment. For further information please contact the publisher.

Tobacco

Mark S. Gold, M.D.

University of Florida Brain Institute
Gainesville, Florida

Plenum Medical Book Company
New York and London

Library of Congress Cataloging-in-Publication Data

On file

ISBN 0-306-44933-1

© 1995 Plenum Press, New York
233 Spring Street, New York, N. Y. 10013
Plenum Medical Book Company is an imprint of Plenum Publishing Corporation

10 9 8 7 6 5 4 3 2 1

Preface

Concern and controversy about the nature of nicotine and the effects of tobacco are constantly in the news. In fact, we may finally be seeing the beginning of the end for one of the most dangerous substances of abuse: nicotine. Despite the fact that reports linking smoking to cancer and heart disease have appeared in the popular and scientific press for three decades, only in the past two years has public opinion turned almost completely against smoking. To be a smoker today is not that far removed from being a leper a century ago.

Today, public opinion about smoking is almost 180 degrees from where it was in 1964, before the Surgeon General's Report was issued that officially linked smoking to a variety of pulmonary and cardiovascular disorders. Today, an overwhelming majority of Americans recognize that nicotine is a dangerous and addicting substance, over two-thirds of Americans favor banning smoking in all public places, and almost 50 percent of Americans would ban cigarettes altogether (*New York Times*/CBS News Survey, April 21, 1994). Even among current smokers, more than 75 percent believe that tobacco companies have been preventing the public from learning the truth about the virulent effects of nicotine and tobacco. This year, the American Medical Association is issuing new guidelines on the diagnosis and treatment of nicotine dependence which stress the physician's role in preventing tobacco use. These guidelines emphasize practice-based and community-based programs which suggest that the doctor must play a key role in leading the fight against smoking.

Over the past decade, our knowledge of the fundamental neurobiological and behavioral processes involved in addiction have contributed to the acceptance of nicotine as a drug whose effects are as powerful as those of cocaine and the opiates. It is the goal of this book, along with the other three volumes in this series, *Marijuana*, *Alcohol*, and *Cocaine*, to present the latest medical information on nicotine and tobacco's neurobiological, physiological, and psychological effects. The history of tobacco use and the latest diagnostic and treatment programs are also presented. In addition, model programs for use by practitioners, developed by the National Cancer Institute and other organizations, are included. Although there has been a decline in tobacco use in some groups, adolescent use still remains at high levels. Adolescents and children are at particular risk, since they are most susceptible to the promotional claims of the tobacco industry and least able to resist the perceived benefits of smoking, both physically and psychologically. Although the tide has clearly turned against tobacco use, the medical profession must approach smoking cessation as seriously as it would approach treatment of any other chronic and life-threatening disease among their patients.

Finally, I would like to thank my students and colleagues at the University of Florida for their regular and critical review of my work and especially William G. Luttge, Ph.D., Chairman, Professor, and Director of the University of Florida Brain Institute, and Dwight Evans, M.D. and Whit Curry, M.D., the Chairs of the Departments of Psychiatry and Community Health and Family Medicine, respectively.

MARK S. GOLD, M.D.

Contents

Chapter 6. Treatment and the Role of the Physician   107

1

Tobacco in the 1990s

Less than two decades ago, cigarette smoking was hardly an antisocial act. It was, in fact, part of the visual definition of sophistication and savoir faire. No one was treated by any sort of health professional for "nicotine dependence" as we now have described in the *Diagnostic and Statistical Manual of Mental Disorders*, Fourth Edition (DSM-IV). The cigarette, cigar, or pipe were the reigning symbols of "the macho man" in the first half of the 20th century. Winston Churchill never appeared without a cigar in his hand, and FDR's cigarette holder was part of an image of good health carefully designed to overcome the reality of his paralysis. Our role models and movie heroes—John Wayne, Humphrey Bogart, Steve McQueen—smoked cigarettes (and, ironically, all died of lung cancer). A cigar after dinner and a cigarette after sex were culturally embedded in our behavior. Marlboro country was the state we all wanted to live in. Smoking was, simply, part of life and linked very strongly to image.

But the times have changed. In the past, the nonsmoker was commonly referred to as a "health nut" and lumped in the same antisocial category as "vegetarians" and others who followed "weird" diets and lifestyles. Today, of course, not eating red meat and not smoking is the *preferred* lifestyle preached by most physicians.

In 1964, when the Surgeon General's Report clearly identified smoking as harmful, a reversal in health behavior began that is almost unprecedented. Antismoking ads became common on radio and television, and eventually cigarette advertising was banned from those media. Other health care movements—to reduce blood pressure, cholesterol, and stress—were a direct result of the success of the antismoking campaigns, which were direct and graphic. Who can forget William Talman, the actor who played the district attorney on Perry Mason, speaking to millions of people "from the grave" about the dangers of smoking, in a commercial that appeared on TV after he died of lung cancer.

Within a decade warning labels appeared on all cigarette packages, and now active antismoking campaigns are mandated in most schools across the country. Most restaurants have designated smoking sections or ban smoking, and lighting up a cigarette around children is socially unacceptable. Most recently, the Pentagon banned smoking from most public and work areas in the military, and large chains such as McDonalds have done the same. The Clinton administration tried to use an increased cigarette tax (from $0.24 now to $0.75 or more) to help pay for its health care package. And for the first time, the FDA, backed by brain and other strong scientific evidence, is trying to have cigarettes classified as a drug, which would severely restrict promotion and access.

Yet millions of Americans continue to smoke, and millions more start smoking each year (Figure 1.1). The tobacco industry is a powerful lobby, with $48 billion in annual revenues. Despite the fact that the Surgeon General reported as long ago as 1988 that nicotine is an addictive substance similar to cocaine or opiates, smoking has leveled off at about 25% of the population. The American Society of Addiction Medicine estimates that in the year 2000, no less than 40 million adults will be active smokers.[1]

Like alcohol, tobacco has always been a part of our history and an important part of our economy, and like alcohol, it is legal

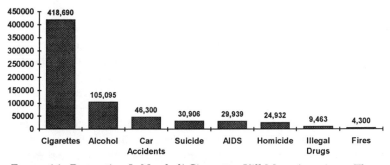

FIGURE 1.1. Prevention Is Needed! Cigarettes Kill More Americans Than AIDS, Accidents, Fires, Illegal Drugs, and Suicides Combined

SOURCE: Centers for Disease Control, U.S. Department of Health and Human Services.

and, despite considerable evidence of its toxic effects, is not regulated by the government in the same manner as marijuana or cocaine.

Why? Because tobacco smoking is, in reality, a social issue, a cultural issue, a political issue, an economic issue, *and* a medical issue with no easy solutions. Smokers don't fit a behavior stereotype, like cocaine or marijuana addicts. Smoking isn't done in secret, like shooting heroin.

As Mark R. Kleiman stated in his book *Against Excess: Drug Policy for Results*:

> Nicotine in tobacco is a health problem, complicated by an addiction problem. This leaves a long list of what nicotine is not. It is not an intoxicant, a behavioral risk (except of addiction), or a source, imagined or real, of great powers or insights. No one commits a crime in a nicotine-induced fury, or wrecks a car in a nicotine-induced daze. No one shows up at work unfit for duty, or at school unable to learn, high on tobacco. . . . no one, not even among those who die of the effects of long-term smoking, bears "tobacco smoker" as a primary social label.

But smokers do seem to fit some sociological stereotypes. Studies indicate that prevalence rates are higher among blacks and Hispanics, blue-collar workers, and people with less education.[2] One expert on drug policy observed that in a typical hospital, it's common to see nurses and orderlies smoking, but very few doctors.[3] It's likely that many of these stereotypical groups of smokers are also targets of heavy promotion on the part of the tobacco industry and the addictiveness of nicotine does the rest.

One of the indisputable facts about tobacco is that its active ingredient, nicotine, is highly addictive. As a 1972 internal memo written by a Phillip Morris executive noted, "no one has ever become a cigarette smoker by smoking without nicotine."[4] That same executive suggested that cigarettes should also be seen as a "dispenser for a dose unit of nicotine."[4] There are in fact, 700 ingredients, many unknown, in cigarettes, but the U.S. Government has admitted publicly that at least five of these are "hazardous" and can be considered carcinogens.[4]

Tobacco use and smoking cigarettes easily meet the criteria established by the Surgeon General, the World Health Organization, and the DSM-IV for drug dependence.[2] Nicotine is, as any smoker or any physician who's treated a smoker can tell you, one of the most virulent of all addictions. It is one of the best examples of the drug stimulating its own taking. There is also considerable evidence that smoking cigarettes is an important "gateway" for adolescent drug abuse. According to Joseph Califano, Jr., the head of the Center on Addiction and Substance Abuse at Columbia University, a study they conducted among teens, ages 12–17, showed that smokers were more than 50 times as likely as nonsmokers to use cocaine and 12 times more likely to use heroin.[5]

Smoking, itself, is one of the most addictive of all human behaviors. A study conducted at the Drug Dependence Research Center of the University of California noted, "Millions of people self-administer nicotine compulsively knowing it might eventually incapacitate or kill. Yet laboratory animals seek nicotine compulsively only when tricked into doing so by their keepers." A recent study showed nicotine withdrawal symptoms exist and can be produced by giving addicted animals antiopiates like naloxone, suggesting a common neuroanatomy for drug taking and frightening similarities between nicotine and opium smoking.

The American Society of Addiction Medicine, in its Public Policy Statement on Nicotine Dependence and Tobacco, identifies nicotine as a psychoactive drug and nicotine dependence as the most common form of chemical dependence in the United States. They further state:

> The general public is aware that tobacco use is harmful, but it seriously underestimates the magnitude of the risks which tobacco poses.
>
> Although the medical profession has traditionally viewed tobacco use as a risk factor for other diseases, and not as a primary problem in itself, this approach has impeded, rather than promoted, the development of optimal treatment methods for patients addicted to nicotine. Nicotine dependence is best regarded as a primary medical problem, with tobacco-related diseases viewed as direct consequences of nicotine dependence. (from *Journal of Addictive Diseases*, 1993;12(1).)

The Facts about Tobacco

Treating tobacco dependence presents one of the most complicated clinical problems a physician will face, first, because of the nature of the addiction and concomitant disorders it produces and, second, because it's a health risk available to anyone of any age.

Overall, smoking, according to the U.S. Surgeon General's office, costs the U.S. over $65 billion per year and "is the only product that when *used as directed* results in death and disability" (Figure 1.2).

According to the Centers for Disease Control and Prevention, a smoker loses seven minutes of life with each cigarette smoked, and *the average smoker smokes 20 cigarettes a day*.[6]

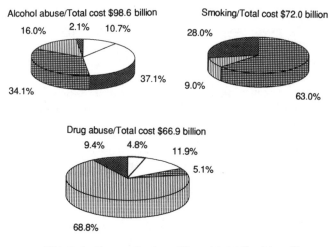

□ Medical □ Illness ⊞ Deaths ⫞ Other related ▨ Special condition

Figure 1.2. The Economic Costs of Substance Abuse

Sources: The Robert Wood Johnson Foundation (1993), and Dorothy P. Rice Institute for Health and Aging, University of California, San Francisco (1990).

The death toll from health problems caused by smoking is staggering, but not surprising. After all, cigarette smoke contains over 1200 chemicals, all harmful to humans: Carbon monoxide is measured at 42,000 parts per million, 840 times the acceptable level in industry. Hydrogen cyanide is found at 160 times the acceptable level.

According to a 1993 study, 20% of all deaths in the United States, almost 419,000, are related to cigarette smoking, and almost 90% of lung cancer deaths are caused by smoking.[7] Still, there are 46 million smokers in the United States who shorten their lives and increase their health risk for lung disease, cancer and heart disease with each puff. Nicotine keeps smokers addicted and smoking despite the consequences to themselves—and others. No matter how educated or sophisticated the smoker is, nicotine can control rational thought. After all, even Freud continued to smoke after he had had surgery for cancer.

Smoking affects not only smokers, but also those who are exposed to smoke through passive inhalation, employers whose smoking workers are sick more often, and the health care system, which bulges from smoking-disorder treatments. Secondhand smoke is classified by the Environmental Protection Agency as a Group A Carcinogen causing cancer in humans.[8] Passive inhalation, according to a 1992 EPA report, causes 3300 lung cancer deaths in people who have never smoked, and 8000–26,000 new pediatric asthma cases. And in infants (birth to 18 months), according to the National Cancer Institute, secondhand smoke is associated with almost 300,000 cases of bronchitis and pneumonia each year.[9] Other studies show that passive smoke causes 10 times as much heart disease as lung disease—making secondhand smoke the third leading cause of preventable death behind active smoking and alcohol.[10]

Smoking in the Workplace

The National Institute for Occupational Safety and Health has recommended banning smoking in the workplace.[11]

The costs of smoking in the workplace are substantial:

- Smokers have a 33%–45% higher absentee rate than non-smokers.
- The average one-pack-plus-per-day smoker, over a lifetime, will cost an employer $624 per year.
- The average smoker costs a company $90 per year in absenteeism.
- Costs in lost productivity account for another $166 per year.
- Lung cancer costs U.S. private industry an estimated $785,500,000 annually.

- The potential dollar savings to U.S. private industry for lung cancer, if all employees were to stop smoking, is estimated at $551,700,000 a year.[12]

In 1989, Pennsylvania passed the Clean Indoor Air Act, requiring employers to (1) develop a policy regulating smoking, (2) post that policy, and (3) provide a copy of the policy to any employee who requests it in order to protect the public health and comfort. Other states have similar laws. Today, it's common to see employees smoking in designated areas or outside in the cold or rain—in effect, social pariahs, isolated from their peers, yet needing to have that cigarette![12] Fortunately, we are living in a time when health risk behavior is becoming more important. Today, most people *must ask permission* to smoke in a public or private place: Restaurants, airplanes, schools, offices and a large number of work sites are now "smoke-free."

Smoking and Children

Beyond the adult health consequences, smoking is a serious threat on several levels to our young. Despite widespread anti-smoking programs, 3 million teenagers smoke on a regular basis, a number that has remained consistent since 1980. Every year a million new teenage smokers light up: 3000 kids a day use a drug that will cause life-long damage. Most of these smokers will have been smoking for several years by the time they graduate from high school (Figure 1.3). And even though it's illegal to sell cigarettes to minors, according to the U.S. Surgeon General the tobacco industry earns $221 million per year in profits from cigarettes sold to children.[13]

The Tobacco Lobby versus the Medical Evidence

One of the most outrageous aspects of cigarette smoking *still* is the promotion of its image. With all of the medical evidence we

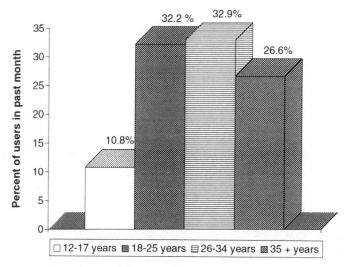

FIGURE 1.3. Prevalence of Cigarette Use

SOURCE: U. S. National Institute of Drug Abuse. National Household Survey on Drug Abuse; Population Estimates 1991. Rockville, MD. DHHS Pub. No. (ABM) 92-1887, 1992.

have about the dangers of smoking, the tobacco companies want us to believe that sophisticated, sexually confident, athletic, healthy, beautiful people smoke and we should too. What boy didn't want to grow up to be like the "Marlboro Man," and what girl didn't want to look like the "Virginia Slims" model with that chic, thin cigarette in her hand! Even small children are not safe. A study published in the *Journal of the American Medical Association* (*JAMA*) revealed that children as young as three years old recognized both the Disney Logo and Old Joe Camel, a cartoon figure promoting Camel cigarettes. What makes this even more disturbing is that Disney is on TV, but cigarettes are advertised only in print media that most three-year-olds can't read! Another study published in *JAMA* then revealed that kids, in fact, were more likely than adults to recognize "Old Joe."

And who can forget candy cigarettes. A study published in *Pediatrics*, demonstrated that when given candy cigarettes, kids didn't eat them but instead "played" with them and associated positive ideas about smoking with them. Many kids admitted that their parents didn't approve of this candy, but they still bought it when they could.

The tobacco lobby is one of the most effective lobbies in Washington. The tobacco industry spends billions per year on advertising, trying to make people think positively about a deadly drug. Through promotion and advertising, people rationalize cigarette use. For example, women widely believe that smoking helps them control their weight, and students believe that nicotine helps them increase their concentration when studying. On one hand, these myths are not without some basis in fact. But just like steroids, which do increase muscle mass, the benefit-to-risk ratio can often be a deadly one.

Yet the industry is largely unregulated by the Food and Drug Administration. The reason, according to Rep. Richard J. Durbin, a member of a congressional coalition trying to give the FDA power to regulate the sale, advertising, and labeling of tobacco products, is that the Congress has never defined tobacco as a food or a drug: "It is nothing short of incredible that the FDA could be involved in a national controversy over whether a spaghetti sauce could use the word 'fresh' on its label . . . and have no jurisdiction over tobacco products which claim to be low-tar, safer, low-nicotine—whatever those words mean." And as Scott Ballin, another coalition member observed, "The FDA has pulled Perrier for containing high levels of benzene, seized orange juice for misleading labeling and established an emergency advisory committee to examine the dangers of silicone breast implants . . . but when it comes to tobacco, the FDA is silent."[14]

It's clear that the media, advertising, and even candy can play a role in the process of becoming a smoker. You can't smell tobacco on a TV screen, makeup can hide yellowed fingers, and a little airbrushing can whiten tobacco-stained teeth. The reality of smoking

can easily be wiped away by the very appealing images bombard-
ing us every day, on billboards, in magazines, and on television.

Cigarettes—Reality Sinks In

There has been a significant decline in smoking. In 1965, 40%
of all adults smoked. By 1987, that number had declined to 26%.[13]
About half the people who tried to quit had done so successfully,
with about 1.3 million people a year giving up smoking because of
overwhelming antismoking efforts from the American Cancer and
Lung Associations, the U.S. Department of Public Health, and so
on. But a survey done by *Prevention Magazine* found that 30% of
adults smoked in 1992, up from 25% the previous year[15] (Figures
1.4 and 1.5).

The idea of legalization of drugs has been raised many times
in this country and has been defeated because most rational people recognize that the only result would be more addicts. The
image of "coke" machines or "pot dispensers" in video arcades or
shopping malls gives parents nightmares. But cigarette machines
are common, and cigarettes can be bought at the supermarket. It's
as easy to get a pack of cigarettes as it is to buy a gallon of milk.

To some extent, the use of illicit substances is controlled by
cost and availability. This is not the case with cigarettes. You can
literally take as high a "dose" of nicotine as you want at any time
for far less than the cost of a gram of cocaine. Taxes may prevent
adolescent use by the nicotine-dependent person, but neither tax
nor high unit cost seems to affect cigarette use. The draw of
nicotine is so strong that wherever supply diminishes or taxes rise
precipitously, a black market is sure to flourish. It's interesting to
note that cigarettes are considered so valuable that they are a
primary unit of barter within the prison system, where cash is
relatively valueless.

There are no simple answers. Tobacco use is entrenched in
our national psyche. It is viewed as a habit—a bad habit—but

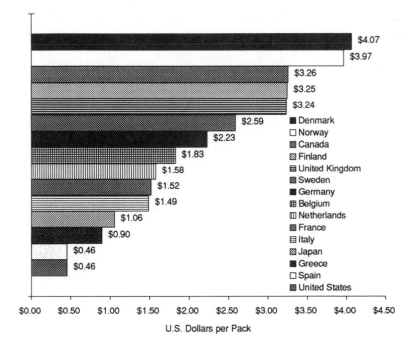

$4.07
$3.97
$3.26
$3.25
$3.24
$2.59
$2.23
$1.83
$1.58
$1.52
$1.49
$1.06
$0.90
$0.46
$0.46

■ Denmark
□ Norway
▨ Canada
▨ Finland
▤ United Kingdom
▧ Sweden
■ Germany
▦ Belgium
▥ Netherlands
▨ France
▤ Italy
▨ Japan
■ Greece
□ Spain
▨ United States

$0.00 $0.50 $1.00 $1.50 $2.00 $2.50 $3.00 $3.50 $4.00 $4.50

U.S. Dollars per Pack

FIGURE 1.4. Comparison of Actual Cigarette Tax Rates in Developed Nations
SOURCE: Coalition on Smoking OR Health.

generally not as an addiction. It is considered by those who smoke a basic right, like freedom of speech or the ability to carry a firearm. Not being exposed to smoking is also viewed as a basic right by non-smokers, whose health is put in jeopardy through no fault of their own. Most people who smoke want to stop, but it is one of the most difficult addictions to break, and one of the most available products on the market. Cigarettes and opium are generally the only drug addictions treated with more of the same drug (the nicotine patch or methadone) and then tapering or detoxify-

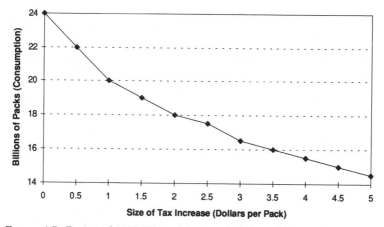

FIGURE 1.5. Projected 1993 (United States) Consumption of Cigarettes at Alternative Tax Levels

Note: This figure projects total 1993 U.S. cigarette consumption based on the following assumptions: (1) estimated price elasticity of demand for cigarettes of −0.4; (2) estimated average 1993 price per pack of $2.16 in the absence of major tax increases, based on historical trends; (3) estimated 1993 (United States) cigarette consumption of 23.418 billion packs in the absence of major tax increases, based on historical trends. For purposes of this illustration, no assumptions were made regarding pricing decisions by manufacturers, wholesalers, and retailers in response to tax increases; such decisions should have a significant effect on price and consumption.

SOURCE: Coalition on Smoking OR Health.

Did You Know?

- 3 million Americans under the age of 21—including 1 out of every 5 high school males—use smokeless tobacco.
- This year 1 out of 5 americans who die will die from tobacco use, killing more than alcohol, car accidents, AIDS, violent crime, heroin, cocaine, and crack combined.
- Tobacco products kill more than 1,100 Americans each day—1 every 75 seconds.
- Raising the tobacco tax 75 cents per pack would save lives, while a $2.00 per pack increase would save an extra 1 million people or 1.9 million lives.
- Canadian experience in raising tobacco taxes has reduced youth smoking by more than 60%.
- Smoking just two cigarettes a day doubles a smoker's risk of lung cancer.

Source: American Cancer Society.

---

ing. From a health standpoint, the answers are clear-cut. But from a social, political, and economic standpoint, we have a long way to go.

References

1. American Society of Addiction Medicine. Public policy statement on nicotine and tobacco. *J Addictive Diseases*. 1993;12(1):141–146.
2. Lee EW, D'Alonzo DO. Cigarette smoking, nicotine addiction, and its pharmacologic treatment. *Arch Intern Med*. 1993;153:34–47.
3. Kleiman MA. *Against Excess*. New York: Basic Books, 1992.
4. Toufexis A. Are smokers junkies? *Time*. March 21, 1994:62.
5. Clymer, A. Expert tells Senate that cigarettes are "entry" to hard drugs. *New York Times*. March 11, 1994.
6. Jarvik ME, Schneider NG. *Nicotine* In Lowinson JH, Ruiz P, Millman RB, Largrod J, eds., *Substance Abuse: A Comprehensive Textbook*. Williams & Wilkins, 1992, pp. 334–356.

7. *Substance Abuse: The Nation's Number One Health Problem: Key Indicators for Policy.* Princeton, NJ: Robert Wood Johnson Foundation, October 1993.
8. *When It Comes to Smoking, A Quitter Always Wins.* Allentown, PA: Coalition for a Smoke-Free Valley, 1993.
9. *I Mind Very Much If You Smoke.* National Cancer Institute, June 1993.
10. Smoking and health review, July–Aug. 1991. In *Smoke-Free Times.* Winter 1993;1(3).
11. Siegel MS. Involuntary smoking in the restaurant workplace. *JAMA.* 1993;270(4):90.
12. *Model Policy for Smoking in the Workplace.* Pennsylvania Department of Health, Division of Health Promotion, Health Risk Reduction Program March, 1989.
13. From the Surgeon General, US Public Health Service. *JAMA.* 1993; 270(7):806.
14. Culhane C. Coalition backs bill to let FDA regulate tobacco. *Am Med News.* June 7, 1993.
15. Smoking increase blots a decade of health gains. *Am Med News.* July 19, 1993.

Additional Sources

Breslau N, Kilbey M, Andreski P. Nicotine dependence, major depression, and anxiety in young adults. *Arch Gen Psychiatr.* 1991;48:1069–1074.

Glassman AH. Cigarette smoking: Implications for psychiatric illness. *Am J Psychiatr.* 1993;150(4):546–553.

Hasenfratz M, Baldinger B, Battig K. Nicotine or tar titration in cigarette smoking behavior. *Psychopharmacology.* 1993;112:253–258.

Kleiman MA. *Against Excess.* New York: Basic Books, 1992.

Let's crack down on smoking. *USA Today.* June 3, 1993.

Levin ED. Nicotinic systems and cognitive function. *Psychopharmacology.* 1992;108:417–431.

Monitoring the Future Study, 1975–1992. NIDA, U.S. Department of Health and Human Services, 1993.

Perkins KA. Effects of tobacco smoking on caloric intake. *Br J Addiction.* 1992;82:193–205.

Perkins KA, Epstein LH, Sexton JE et al. Effects of nicotine on hunger and eating in male and female smokers. *Psychopharmacology.* 1992;106:53–59.

Persico AM. Persistent decrease in heart rate after smoking cessation: A 1-year follow-up study. *Psychopharmacology*. 1992;106:397–400.

Pomerleau CS, Garcia AW, Pomerleau OF et al. The effects of menstrual phase and nicotine abstinence on nicotine intake and on biochemical and subjective measures in women smokers: A preliminary report. *Psychoneuroendocrinology*. 1992;17(6):627–638.

Siegel M. Involuntary smoking in the restaurant workplace: A review of employee exposure and health effects. *JAMA*. July 18, 1993;270(4):490.

Smoke Free Times Newsletter. Winter 1993;1(3).

Smoking burns body fat. *American Medical News*. January 24–31, 1994.

Smoking increase blots a decade of health gains. *Am Med News*. July 19, 1993.

Snider M. EPA panel: Passive smoke toxic. *USA Today*. July 23, 1992.

Substance Abuse: The Nation's Number One Health Problem: Key Indicators for Policy. Princeton NJ: Robert Wood Johnson Foundation, October 1993.

2

Tobacco

A Short History of the American Economy

How did we get to this point in American history where our health care system allows a drug like nicotine, which kills over 400,000 people a year, to be dispensed legally—and to almost anyone? How can the most advanced health care system in the most affluent nation in the world ignore a public health threat currently far more dangerous than AIDS? Or, even more perplexing, how can we allow a dangerous drug that can lead to heart disease, lung cancer, and a myriad of other fatal diseases to be promoted to our children through clever advertising and promotion?

The answer is in the economics of the tobacco industry and the virulent tug of the product itself—an almost perfect package designed to reinforce its own use. To understand this confluence of sociology and neurochemistry, one has to understand a lot more about the history of the tobacco industry—and how we came to our love affair with tobacco. Without this perspective, few physicians will be able to effectively treat tobacco addiction and its concomitant diseases.

America and the companies that make cigarettes are so intertwined that one cannot actually study American history without studying the rise of the tobacco industry. In fact, it can be said that the tobacco industry can trace its roots to the day that Christopher Columbus stepped off the boat and was handed a pipe by the natives.

From the first colonies in Virginia to the present day, a large part of the success of the American economy has been based on tobacco. Before cotton was king, there was tobacco farming, which, many sociologists have argued, gave rise to plantations and the need for slaves in the South, and to the Civil War. And then, after the war, it salvaged the economy of the "new South."

When Columbus first set foot in the New World in San Salvador in 1492, the natives presented him with "dry leaves," which Columbus assumed "must be a thing very much appreciated by them."[1] But it's almost certain that the Native Americans were smoking tobacco in a variety of forms long before Columbus sailed to the Americas. Columbus and his men reported that the natives "drank smoke." But unfortunately, the Spanish sailors and their Portuguese leaders failed to heed the early warning signs. Several "drank" so much smoke that they literally couldn't stop. One of Columbus's men, Redrego de Jerez, was so possessed by tobacco that he was eventually imprisoned by the Spanish Inquisition for his "devilish habit."[1]

But the Spanish weren't alone. Amerigo Vespucci and Jacques Cartier, who explored the mainland and Canada, also described natives drying and chewing tobacco, mixing it with lime, and smoking it in a pipe.

Tobacco was, in fact, the first export from the New World, thus launching the economic juggernaut that has, to this day, continued almost unchallenged. And in fact, it was first billed as an anxiolytic. Once the Spanish brought tobacco seeds back to Europe, tobacco was cultivated and prescribed as a cure for stress, ulcers, headaches, asthma, and even rheumatism.

As a result of its seeming medicinal value, tobacco quickly became an object of scientific study. It owes its botanical name,

Nicotiana, to Jean Nicot, the French ambassador to Portugal, who was so convinced of tobacco's medicinal value that he sent some tobacco seeds to the royal family in France. The popularity of tobacco as a "wonder drug" quickly spread, as well as its use for recreational purposes, although many users rationalized that they were smoking to "ward off the plague."

The Spanish and French quickly understood that they had a valuable cash commodity on their hands and began serious cultivation and importation of tobacco. Although among the last Europeans to discover tobacco, the British, led by famous sea captains such as Sir Francis Drake and Sir Walter Raleigh, soon joined the tobacco industry. The explorers, who became smokers during their exploits in the West Indies, brought tobacco back to England as a gift for the British court. Raleigh, who later established the colony of Virginia, also helped launch tobacco farming there, thus creating an economic base that still relies on tobacco today.

The British, however, weren't as ready as other Europeans to embrace smoking despite the growing demand for tobacco in England. As its popularity and nonmedical use grew, concern increased, and King James I published "A Counterblaste to Tobacco" in 1604, which described smoking as "A custome lothsome to the eye, hatefull to the Nose, harmefull to the braine, [and] dangerous to the Lungs."

Like all issues having to do with tobacco, the economics were probably an underlying factor, since at that time tobacco was largely being imported from Spain (historically an enemy of England), at great expense to the British. But once Raleigh developed the colonial tobacco farms in Virginia, the English attitude changed. The "official" start of the tobacco industry in North America actually can be traced to 1612, when John Rolfe, an English colonist, brought tobacco seeds to Virginia from South America. He and others soon realized that the climate and soil in Virginia were excellent for growing tobacco. As the other southern colonies were settled, the tobacco plant followed quickly, and it became one of the most important crops not only in Virginia but also throughout the South.

When the first shipment of Virginia-grown tobacco was sent to Britain in 1616, British entrepreneurs quickly realized that the quality was superior, and soon British tobacco was outselling that imported from Spain. Still, in spite of the king's efforts to discourage the burgeoning Virginia tobacco industry through high taxes, the colony flourished.

Although smoking was the most popular means of using tobacco, the use of snuff, a powdered form of tobacco which was pinched between the fingers or sniffed from the back of the hand, producing a sneeze, became very popular among the upper classes in Europe by the end of the 17th century. Even British royalty used snuff. However, this type of tobacco use declined in popularity after the French Revolution, when it became associated with the decadence of the ousted aristocracy, a "thing of the past."

Despite its almost instant popularity in Europe, tobacco was not embraced as readily by the people in other countries, although few cultures rejected it outright. Only religious views, which applied to an overall view of lifestyle, seemed to slow its spread. For example, tobacco was considered intoxicating in Muslim countries, a direct violation of the teachings of the Koran, and those who smoked were punished severely. Smokers in Asian countries such as Japan, China, and Russia were also severely punished. However, the punishments had little effect on tobacco's popularity, and it became common for governments to admonish smoking yet make a handsome profit by levying high taxes on tobacco.

Chewing tobacco is a uniquely American contribution to tobacco use. Although Native Americans had always chewed tobacco, Americans embraced it at the beginning of the 19th century, in large part as a statement of nationalism and a repudiation of the aristocracy of Europe. After all, the privileged classes used snuff. One Englishman suggested that "the national emblem of the United States be a spittoon rather than an eagle."[1] By the late 1890s, chewing tobacco probably accounted for half of all tobacco consumed in the United States.[2]

As European explorers pushed west and into Central and South America, they found smoking to be common. The first

TOBACCO

21

forms of "cigarette" smoking were reported among Mexican Indians by the Spanish, who told of how they smoked tobacco through hollow reeds. But smoking tobacco rolled in lightweight paper did not become popular until the 1840s, when it became the rage in France, especially among French women. Around this time, a new kind of tobacco, a low-nicotine, mild, sweet type well suited to cigarette smoking, was first grown in North Carolina. Thus, the era of competition among tobacco growers began in earnest. The race for the hearts and lungs of Americans was on for good.

England, obviously, was the American colonies' most important trading partner, with most American tobacco being exported to England until the Revolutionary War. After independence was won, the newly formed United States began producing smoking tobacco, chewing tobacco, and snuff for domestic use, and cigars were manufactured in the early 1800s.

As in England, there was a small but vocal antismoking movement in the nascent United States. Although European doctors raised concerns about the recreational use of tobacco in the 1500s, and the Puritans thought of it as a dangerous narcotic, the antismoking movement in the United States can trace its real roots to Dr. Benjamin Rush, the founder of the Temperance Union, who, in 1798, made a connection between the use of liquor and tobacco. Rush believed that tobacco created a craving for "strong drinks."[1] In countless pamphlets and speeches, he condemned tobacco as immoral and unhealthy. However, Rush was, as almost all antismoking movements have been, ultimately unsuccessful and tobacco use continued to flourish throughout the 18th and 19th centuries.

Although there are reports of hand-rolled cigarettes being smoked in the 1600s, smoking tobacco in cigarette form did not really gain popularity until the Industrial Revolution took hold. Along with a wide variety of labor-saving devices, the first cigarette-making machine was invented in the early 1880s and by 1885, according to one expert, over 1 billion cigarettes per year were being sold.[2]

Interestingly, some of the more intense antismoking efforts have also been economically inspired. When cigarettes, or "little cigars," were finally mass-produced, alarms rang not only for those who saw tobacco as the demise of morality but also by the cigar industry, which saw a real threat to its profits. It made claims that cigarettes contained opium and morphine, arsenic and lead.[1] But cigarettes were here to stay and today are still the most popular form of tobacco used.

Tobacco use continued into the 20th century, relatively untouched, until the 1960s, when the U.S. Surgeon General's Report, for the first time, linked smoking with cancer and other diseases in an almost indisputable scientific report. In 1971, the Royal College of Physicians of London issued a similar report. The result, however, was not the end of smoking. Instead, the industry received what most health care professionals consider a simple "slap on the wrist."

Since 1966, all tobacco manufacturers have been required to place a health warning on all packages and cartons of cigarettes, and in 1971, Congress passed a law banning cigarette advertising on radio and television. The 1989 Surgeon General's Report linked smoking with lung and throat cancers, emphysema, and heart disease. The evidence against smoking mounts year by year, yet the tobacco industry remains untouched. Why?

As the history of the United States has shown, tobacco and the U.S. economy are inextricably linked, and in 1995 it is not that much different from 1794. Today, North Carolina grows more tobacco than any other state, but Tennessee, South Carolina, Virginia, Georgia, Maryland, Pennsylvania, and Florida all provide income and jobs related to tobacco. The United States is one of the leading tobacco-growing countries in the world. Phillip Morris is the largest tobacco company in America and the largest consumer-products company in the world, and Marlboro cigarettes, a product of Phillip Morris, is the best-selling packaged product in the world.[3] According to journalist Roger Rosenblatt in an article in the *New York Times* (March 20, 1994), "The connection of the company to the American economy is so deep and secure that if one were to remove Philip Morris without first finding something equally valuable to fill the hole, much of the country would cave in."

Rosenblatt reports that Philip Morris is the largest taxpayer in the country, paying $4.5 billion in taxes in 1992; provides $4 billion toward the balance of payments; employs 161,000 people worldwide, not including those people involved on the periphery of tobacco, such as those who make filters and papers for cigarettes; gives more than $50 million to tax-exempt organizations; and is one of the largest advertisers in the world (it spent over $2 billion on media advertising in 1992). Cigarette advertising is one of the biggest revenue sources for magazines.

In addition, the tobacco industry gave $2.39 million to Congress in 1991–1992. Even health care companies and institutions reap benefits from the tobacco companies, producing nicotine patches to help people stop smoking and fungicides to help tobacco farmers grow more tobacco. The board of directors for Phillip Morris reads like a Who's Who of American Business and Influence. One member of the board, John S. Reed, also sits on the board of Memorial Sloan-Kettering Cancer Center in New York City.

Like King James centuries before, for years Members of Congress and antismoking groups, even the U.S. Surgeon General, have advocated raising taxes on cigarettes.[4] According to former Representative Mike Synar (D-Okla.), "I think pricing is one of the best ways to keep this product out of the hands of children . . . I wouldn't mind seeing it go to $5.00 a pack." (Charles Culhane, "Coalition Backs Bill to Let FDA Regulate Tobacco", *American Medical News*, June 7, 1993). No matter what is tried, current smokers somehow will get their hands on their drug. For example, when the State of Maryland raised the cigarette tax by 20 cents per pack, the number of smokers dropped by 20%—according to sales figures. However, many people believe that smokers from Maryland are simply crossing the border into neighboring states where cigarettes are much cheaper. Some experts believe that even at $5.00 per pack, nicotine addicts would still smoke. Even the homeless seem to find the money for cigarettes! President Clinton hoped to finance a portion of his health care plan through a large increase in the U.S. cigarette tax. Others have advocated raising the minimum age to purchase cigarettes from 18 to 21, eliminating government subsidies and assistance which encourage tobacco production, strengthening warning labels on cigarettes, promoting more research into tobacco, and perhaps, most damaging to the tobacco industry, classifying nicotine as a drug, with the safety issues that entails.

Is it realistic to expect smoking to be banned? Probably not. While there has been a resurgence in calls to make illicit drugs legal (e.g., marijuana), Americans tend to view cigarette smoking and illicit drug use as totally separate issues. Therefore, sociological trends don't seem to affect cigarette smoking. However, it is being viewed more and more as a health issue for adults and a serious health issue for young people.

But it is within the realm of possibility to increasingly stigmatize users, treat addicts, and enact and enforce laws that can begin to limit the use of tobacco in the future. Many companies have already voluntarily done so. Legislation has been proposed to make tobacco companies document their health claims and to be banned from sponsoring sports and cultural events. And recent polls show strong public support for more regulation of the tobacco companies. Can health concerns win out over economic ones? It is an age-old conflict that has existed throughout our history. Twenty-five percent of Americans smoke. Most, when surveyed, would like to quit if they could. Hopefully, we have reached a point in our history when we recognize addiction as addiction and drugs as drugs and will do something to change it.

References

1. McKim WA, *Drugs and Behavior*. Englewood Cliffs, NJ: Prentice Hall, 1986.
2. Schlaadt RG, Shannon PT, *Drugs of Choice*. Englewood Cliffs, NJ: Prentice-Hall, 1986.

3. Rosenblatt R, How do tobacco executives live with themselves. *New York Times*, March 20, 1994, pp. 34–39, 55, 73–76.
4. From the Surgeon General, US Public Health Service. *JAMA*, 1993, 270(7):806.

Additional Source

Tobacco. *World Book Encyclopedia*, Vol 19, 1987, pp. 240–244.

3

The Neurobiological
Effects of Tobacco

Cigarette smoking is such a virulent, habitual behavior that reversal occurs in less than 10% of those who try every year. Fully one-third of all smokers try to stop each year—and fail. Whether patients seek professional medical assistance or attend nonprofessional, popular programs, their chances of complete success are about the same as if they "decide" to stop on their own.

Smoking is recognized by virtually every segment of the health care community as one of the most self-destructive behaviors known today. But as the last two chapters clearly illustrate, clinicians will continue to see myriad groups of patients who present significant symptoms directly related to the effects of tobacco, nicotine, and cigarette smoke.

Cigarettes, some say, when used as directed by the manufacturer, are the most lethal product available for peacetime use in the United States. About 30% of people who smoke die directly from complications of this addictive substance, despite the fact that cigarettes are smoked with great regularity in the absence of profound euphoria or withdrawal compared to other psychoactive substances.

The reasons behind this extraordinary quandary lie in the nature of addictive behavior, and in the fact that the neurobiological mechanisms of our brains are undefended targets for nicotine. The combination of nicotine, which is both an agonist and an antagonist, and the carcinogenic properties contained in cigarette smoke create a product more deadly than any viral agent or immunological threat encountered to date.

Yet, amazingly, tobacco remains legal and easily obtainable by the population segment—adolescents—most likely to have such a strong biological response that their lifelong use is facilitated.

Tobacco's basic effects are both behavioral and neurobiological. Therefore, the most important weapon that any clinician can employ is a clear understanding of the combination of behavioral changes determined by a variety of neurobiological actions that occur during tobacco use.

A Common Neuroanatomy of Reward
for Drugs of Abuse

Responding to the need for a greater comprehension of addiction, researchers have attempted to discover commonalities in the addiction, reinforcement, and withdrawal processes for a variety of drugs. This research has been complicated by the fact that each drug of abuse has multiple actions, including many that appear to be contradictory. Addictive drugs are often taken in combination with other drugs and/or alcohol, and in environments that are difficult to duplicate in the laboratory (Figure 3.1).

Nevertheless, a common neuroanatomy for all drugs of abuse has been proposed. It would appear from various studies that recent research has identified common neuronal reward circuits and even intracellular changes associated with chronic morphine and cocaine administration which can serve as a model for study.

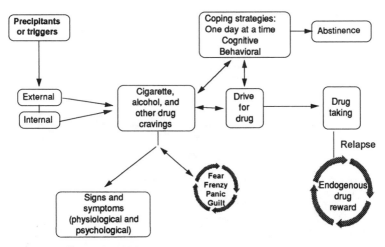

FIGURE 3.1. Nicotine Reward versus Abstinence

Nicotine, it seems, is a prime candidate to be included in the list of substances of abuse that fit the model.

Among the common "traits" nicotine dependence shares with other psychoactive substances is its ability to cause changes in brain function gradually over time, in response to prolonged periods of exposure. Gradually these become fixed in the brain. These changes persist for extended periods of time after discontinuation of chronic nicotine administration. These so-called adaptive changes, referred to as tolerance or a reduction in the drug's effects, require, as do other drugs, repeated administration or the need to increase the dose to maintain the same effect (Figure 3.2).

Nicotine also provokes "sensitization or reverse tolerance," where a constant drug dose elicits increased effects. Addiction, which follows, is the accumulation of tolerance, sensitization, and dependence seen in humans as compulsive drug use despite adverse consequences. Such a dissociation between drug-taking, smoking, and reason suggests that drug-related changes in the brain are critically important in maintaining addiction.

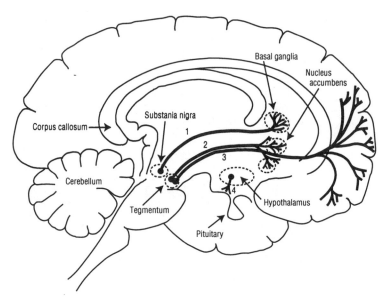

FIGURE 3.2. Principle Dopaminergic Tracts

SOURCE: R. E. Hales and S. C. Yudofsky. *Textbook of Neuropsychiatry*. ©1987 American Psychiatric Press. Used with permission.

Nicotine addiction, like other addictions, is defined by a drug-induced brain change which presumably can be studied in animals to generate neural change models, and once these changes are understood, new treatments can be tried in these animal models. Investigators are constantly looking for changes that nicotine produces in the brain that cause addiction and possibly specific interactions between genetic and environmental factors that make certain animals or people more likely to become addicts. Studies have focused on the noradrenergic locus coeruleus, after its role in the physiological or autonomic aspects of opiate withdrawal were reported and studied in great detail in 1978, and on the mesolimbic dopamine reward system. While studies of nicotine are in their infancy relative to the studies of opiates and cocaine, by reviewing these studies we should be able to understand nicotine dependence as a combination of drug reward, conditioning, and "host factors."

Looking at the lessons learned from these extensive studies of animals and humans during chronic opioid or cocaine administration and discontinuation, we assume similarities which have not been proven by direct study. However, the study of the behavior or detailed molecular mechanisms by which the drugs produce the altered biochemical and electrophysiological phenotypes can help us understand the molecular basis of drug action and the interaction of the drug, genes, and environment.

Reward and Reinforcement

A thorough understanding of the neuroanatomical substrates for addiction requires a discussion of how drug use results both from seeking drugs (reinforcement) and avoiding withdrawal (pharmacological dependence). This area is the subject of many ongoing studies that attempt to understand the relationship of withdrawal and reinforcement, since the two may not be independent phenomena. Or does one lead to the other? Can avoidance of withdrawal drive one to use more and more dangerous drugs? And what is the relevance of all of this to nicotine and tobacco use?

Several studies have confirmed the comorbidity of various substances of abuse. The Epidemiological Catchment Area (ECA) study found that 16% of the general population experienced alcoholism at some point during their lifetime. Of these alcoholics, 30% also suffered from other drug dependence. Similarly, the rates of alcohol dependence among other drug addicts were high: 36% of cannabis addicts, 62% of amphetamine addicts, 67% of opiate addicts, and 84% of cocaine addicts were also alcoholics. These studies, combined with clinical observations regarding the concurrent use of multiple substances, suggest common biological determinants.[1]

Responding to the need for both stimulant and opiate investigation and for a greater comprehension of addiction, several researchers have attempted to discern commonalities in the reinforcement, addiction, and withdrawal processes for a variety of drugs. A thorough understanding of these processes requires a discussion of how drug use results both from seeking drugs (reinforcement) and avoiding withdrawal (pharmacological dependence). The clinical implications of reinforcement and withdrawal will be discussed in detail.

Reinforcement

In the 1950s, researchers suggested that addiction-prone drugs activated brain reinforcement circuits. Since that time, studies have confirmed that all drugs of abuse/addiction:

- Either enhance brain stimulation reinforcement or lower brain reinforcement thresholds
- Affect brain reinforcement circuits either through basal neuronal firing and/or basal neurotransmitter discharge
- Will cause animals to work for injections into the brain reinforcement area but not for injections into other areas of the brain
- Will have their reinforcement properties significantly mediated by blockades of the brain reinforcement system either through lesions or pharmacological methods[2]

The medial forebrain bundle (MFB) region of the brain, together with the nuclei and projection fields of the MFB, have been found to be primarily responsible for the positive reinforcement associated with drugs of addiction. Histofluorescence-mapping techniques have revealed a close association between the brain stimulation reinforcement region and the mesotelencephalic dopamine (DA) system. Additional studies have confirmed the importance of DA neurotransmission to brain reinforcement.[3] While the initial hypothesis suggested that electrical brain stimulation reinforcement directly triggered DA neurotransmission, it is now believed that the activation of the DA neurons occurs as a convergence following activation of a myelinated caudally running fiber system whose neurons lack the properties associated with DA neurons.[4] Drugs of abuse and addiction enhance brain reinforcement through their actions upon this DA convergence (Figure 3.3).

Species-specific survival drives, such as eating, drinking, copulation, and seeking shelter, are positive reinforcers. Drugs of abuse and addiction are also positive reinforcers. The fundamental element in animal responses to these survival drives appears to be forward locomotion. In fact, the forward locomotion response apparently results from a number of drugs, including cocaine, amphetamine, opiates, barbiturates, benzodiazepines, alcohol, nicotine, caffeine, cannabis, and phencyclidine.[5] Specifically, these positive reinforcement drugs of abuse and addiction appear to share a common effect upon DA systems.

Stimulant Reinforcement

Amphetamine and cocaine achieve positive reinforcement by blocking the reuptake of DA into the presynaptic neuron.[6] By preventing DA reuptake, greater concentrations of DA remain in the synaptic cleft with more DA available at the postsynaptic site for stimulation of specific receptors. The abnormally high levels of DA in the synapse inhibits the firing rate of dopaminergic cells and mediates the process by which synaptic DA is inactivated. Numerous studies have supported the positive reinforcement effects associated with increased synaptic levels of DA.[6] Nicotine has also been found to enhance DA levels and to be a positive reinforcer, although not to the same extent as cocaine. DA release in the nucleus accumbens has occurred in vitro in response to small concentrations of nicotine.[7] This DA effect of nicotine may explain the addictive power of tobacco.

While the above information concentrates on the pharmacological effects of addictive drugs in the reinforcement process,

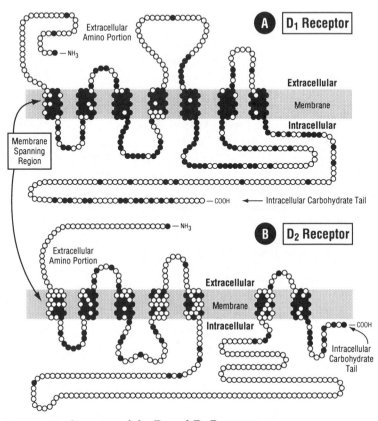

FIGURE 3.3. Structure of the D_1 and D_2 Receptors

SOURCE: Adapted from B. F. O'Dowd. "Structures of Dopamine Receptors." *J Neurochem.* 1993;60:810. ©1993 Raven Press, Ltd. Used with permission.

other factors may lead to positive reinforcement. For example, drug use may enhance a user's social standing, encourage approval by drug-using friends, and convey a special status to the user. Even in poverty-riddled environments, smokers have been known to trade valuable commodities for cigarettes.

Reinforcement Leads to Learning

As demonstrated above, cocaine, opiates, and nicotine, on a basic or primitive level, produce rapid reinforcement described as a sense of well-being. This reinforcement is clearly neurobiological in that the drug use stimulates its own taking and produces an imperceptible sense of organismic accomplishment similar to species-specific survival behaviors. Drug users feel as if they have acted to preserve the species, when in reality they have simply bypassed the normal behavior reinforcement system.

The changes in mood associated with drug reinforcement serve as an unconditioned stimulus. Given frequent association with these changes, a variety of other factors, including the psychological (mood states, cognitive expectations of euphoria, stress, etc.) and the environmental (drug paraphernalia, drug-using locations or friends, etc.), can become conditioned stimuli. Exposure to these conditioned stimuli can precipitate withdrawal-like physiological responses that the user interprets as drug cravings and that often lead to relapse.

Nicotine and Withdrawal

While significant evidence supports the role of dopamine in the reinforcement process, the neuroanatomy of withdrawal is not as clearly defined. However, a wide variety of dependence-producing drugs, with apparently little in common pharmacologically, share common withdrawal effects associated with the locus coeruleus (LC). Support for a shared withdrawal pathway also stems from similarities in withdrawal treatments: Opiates, benzodiazepines, nicotine, and alcohol have all had their withdrawal symptoms treated effectively by clonidine, a medication that suppresses LC hyperactivity.[8]

Normally, the LC is activated by pain, blood loss, and cardiovascular collapse, but not by nonthreatening stimuli.[9] However, in the opiate-dependent animal, withdrawal precipitation clears opiates from the mu receptor and places neurons in the LC in a state of hyperexcitability (also referred to as rebound from chronic inhibition or LC hyperactivity).[10] The resultant noradrenergic hyperactivity and release appear to be an essential factor in the precipitation of withdrawal symptoms and signs.

Unlike in opiate and alcohol withdrawal, symptoms of tobacco and cocaine withdrawal can be relatively mild and transient.[11] Chronic cocaine administration has been shown to decrease brain levels of DA and norepinephrine (NE) while inhibiting LC activity.[12] One might expect that abstinence in nicotine-dependent people would trigger LC activity and subsequent withdrawal symptoms in a manner similar to opiate withdrawal. The intense craving and high recidivism rate associated with cocaine use appears to derive more from a drive state than from the avoidance of withdrawal discomfort.

Nicotine withdrawal is associated with physiological, behavioral, and subjective changes, including decreased adrenaline, cortisol, heart rate, thyroid function, tremor, increased taste for sweets, resting metabolic rate, weight, metabolism of several drugs, and slowing of the EEG.

The behavioral effects include decreased performance, especially on vigilance tasks, and increased aggression and caloric intake (especially sweet–fat combinations). Irritability, restlessness, and insomnia are regularly reported by patients during acute nicotine abstinence. With the exception of decreased heart rate and increased eating and weight gain, the signs and symptoms of nicotine withdrawal overlap with many reported from sedative, opioid, and cocaine abstinence.[13]

Nicotine withdrawal appears to the physician observer to be less severe than alcohol or opioid withdrawal. However, on the basis of relapse rate, it is difficult to state with certainty which is the most severe withdrawal. Hughes has noted that some smokers will experience greater withdrawal from nicotine than some addicts experience from cessation of opioids or other drugs.[14]

Nicotine withdrawal severity does not appear to be directly related to duration or dose of nicotine or even the number of cigarettes per day. Even nicotine and cotinine levels have not always predicted the severity of nicotine withdrawal. Withdrawal signs and symptoms can become conditioned to environmental events so that smoking-related stimuli provoke an increased heart rate.

Most nicotine withdrawal effects begin 6–12 hours after cessation of nicotine, with a peak at 1–3 days, and last 3–4 weeks, with nearly 40% of smokers having withdrawal symptoms that last more than 3–4 weeks. Many nicotine-dependent persons do not have withdrawal complaints. Similarly, many other addicts of cocaine or sedatives do not complain of withdrawal. In comparisons to other drug withdrawal states, nicotine withdrawal has a time course similar to alcohol or heroin, but without the extremes of DTs, vomiting, and so forth. Nicotine remains among the most addictive of drugs.[14] While protracted withdrawal is reported for alcohol, opioids, and stimulants, nicotine withdrawal appears to have hunger, weight gain, and nicotine craving as prominent protracted withdrawal symptoms.[15]

Clearly, nicotine withdrawal follows from stopping cigarettes or cessation of other nicotine-containing products and is reversed by nicotine polacrilex or transdermal nicotine.

In animals, nicotine withdrawal is demonstrated in studies of operant behavior and by increased eating and decreased motor activity. In animals, nicotine withdrawal also effectively mimics anxiety states. While the evidence points to nicotine's role in dependence, tolerance and withdrawal, the exact neuroanatomy and neuropharmacology of withdrawal are not clear. Naloxone has been used to provoke opioid withdrawal and even to diagnose opioid dependence. No such pharmacological test or procedure exists for nicotine.

Two other important points regarding nicotine withdrawal are:

- Data suggest that infants of smoking mothers do not appear to have withdrawal, and nonhuman studies do not demonstrate withdrawal.
- Whether relapse to smoking is related to withdrawal symp-

toms or craving is not clear, but recent studies suggest that smokers who gain more weight after cessation are less likely to relapse

Clinical Implications

In fact, for all drugs, *reinforcement* may be more important than withdrawal in the persistence of addiction and relapse, since successful treatment of withdrawal has not generally improved treatment retention and recovery. All addiction-prone drugs are used, at least initially, for their positive effects and because the user believes the short-term benefits of this experience surpass the long-term costs. Once initiated, drug use permits access to the reinforcement system, which is believed to be anatomically distinct from the negative/withdrawal system in the LC and elsewhere.[16] This reinforcement system, accessed now by exogenous self-administration by drugs of addiction, provides users with an experience which their brain equates with profoundly important events like eating, drinking, and sex.

Tolerance may occur when the brain environment redefines "normal" and resets neurochemical homeostasis. If a brain bathed in two packs of nicotine per day becomes the new neural "normal," it should not be surprising that relapse and drug use are the rule rather than the exception. If drugs are taken because of drive states, they develop a life of their own as the brain redefines normal to require their presence in expected quantities.[17]

Drug use becomes an acquired drive state which permeates all aspects of human life. Withdrawal from drug use activates separate neural pathways, which cause withdrawal events to be perceived as life-threatening, and the subsequent physiological and psychological reactions often lead to renewed drug consumption. The treatment research consensus that early intervention, early treatment, time in treatment, and/or abstinence are the greatest predictors of treatment success thus reflects the time required to reinstate pre-drug neural homeostasis, fading of drug reinforcement behavior patterns and conditioned cues, and the reemergence of endogenous reinforcement for work, friends, shelter, food, water, and copulation.[18]

With the exception of methadone and naltrexone, the current pharmacological treatments for drug abuse/addiction—including desipramine, bromocriptine, fluoxetine, and clonidine—rely primarily upon the alleviation of withdrawal symptoms. While these medications have helped some patients facilitate the transformation from addiction to a drug-free state, the frequency of relapse experienced by most addicts suggests the importance of reinforcement in encouraging future drug use.

Drug reinforcement is so powerful that even when it is eliminated by pharmacological blockade (e.g., naltrexone), humans quickly identify themselves as "opiate unavailable" and nonreceptive. While under pharmacological blockade, humans will change their behavior (i.e., stop taking opiates). Without additional treatment, their attachment to the drug and its effects remains unchanged. Once an antagonist is discontinued, the untreated addict continues self-administration. These data are in agreement on the difficulties of lasting suppression of drug self-administration behavior.[19]

Aversive conditioning and systematic deconditioning have been similarly disappointing since the effects of drug stimuli are well known and well remembered by the addict. For example, contingency incarceration programs where probationers with drug offenses face a return to prison upon relapse have not proven to be an effective deterrent to drug use.[20] However, reduced probation time was shown to be a reinforcer.[21] Even medical practitioners facing the loss of their professional license did not totally prevent relapse to cocaine and opiate abuse.[22]

The failure of aversive conditioning in the treatment of drug addiction is logical, given the assumption that the brain emphasizes the positive reinforcement of survival behaviors such as eating, drinking, and sex while deemphasizing the hostility of the environment. Reinstatement of drive states appears more persistent than memory for pain or dysphoria. Memory is highly state-dependent, and access to memories while intoxicated may be severely limited to similar intoxication states. Reinforcement of drive states is naturally more important than a real risk of some future consequences from drug use.

Extinction treatment was thought to be of potential benefit if addicts were forced to use heroin in the presence of a naltrexone blockade or to perform nonreinforced drug self-administration. However, studies where addicts were encouraged to perform their drug use ritual in the laboratory and to use heroin during active blockade demonstrated a state-dependent extinction.[23] But, since extinguished response could be readily reinstated upon discontinuation of naltrexone, usefulness in treatment was limited.

Clearly, relapse prevention and successful treatment for addiction require much more than the alleviation of withdrawal symptoms. It is well known that patients with higher pretreatment levels of social supports, employment, and productivity have a better prognosis for successful response to initial treatment and long-term abstinence.[18] Treatment outcome for these patients may improve because these patients perceive the long-term cost of drug use (loss of family or job) as outweighing the short-term "benefit" of drug use. Educational efforts that mobilize the family, employer, and friends, while stressing the risks associated with drugs, help individuals to stop or avoid drug use.

Behavioral Manifestations of Reinforcement

Animal studies using microdialysis show that a conditioned response can provoke an increase in dopamine levels in the nucleus accumbens, in effect a "priming dose" that may enhance desire for the drug.[24] O'Brien has studied the responses of addicts to videos of people using their drug of choice. These videos have been found to provoke craving and arousal, measured by increases in blood pressure and heart rate, and by decreases in skin

temperature and skin resistance, that are very similar to the response from using cocaine or another stimulant.[24]

Nicotine and Its Neurobiological Effects

How does all of the above fit with the specific neurobiological
scenario created by nicotine?

Researchers have been studying the effects of nicotine on the
brain for over 100 years,[25] specifically nicotine's effects on the
sympathetic nervous system, and the resultant blockage of neurotransmission through the autonomic ganglia.[26] One initial finding,
which has since been reconfirmed over a century, is that a lower
dose of nicotine stimulates neurotransmission, while a higher
dose creates synaptic blockage. Nicotine, it is now clear, acts in
a paradoxical fashion that is dose-dependent and is unlike all of
the other drugs of abuse, in this respect, even though it produces
the same basic reward-reinforcing drive.

Nicotine follows a variety of neurological pathways that control reward, pleasure, and stimulation within the central nervous
system that are at the heart of the lure of tobacco.[27] This system is
also at the root of nicotine's agonist and antagonist properties.

There are significant patterns of nicotinic receptors located
throughout the central and peripheral nervous systems, the autonomic ganglia, and the striated muscle at the neuromuscular
junction. Nicotine's multiple effects and actions occur because
nicotine's action at each receptor site is different and the receptor's
binding effects are also diverse.[25]

For example, some of nicotine's behavioral effects are derived
from its effects at nicotine-acetylcholinergic receptors (nAchRs)
throughout the hippocampus, the midbrain, and the nucleus
accumbens. It's likely that most of the reinforcing and reward
stimulating effects occur at the nucleus accumbens, where ventral
tegmental dopamine neurons are located.[27–29]

Central among those behavioral effects is the locomotor stimulation that many smokers report. Studies indicate that, most

likely, the D1, D2, D3, and D4 dopamine receptors become involved in the stimulation of locomotor activity once dopamine is released in the striatum and nucleus accumbens. Further studies also show that there may be an additive effect that is a result of environmental stimuli.[30]

Another question that has arisen as nicotine's dopaminergic effects are studied is whether the level of locomotor effect is dose-dependent. Since many smokers use tobacco throughout the day and at fairly consistent levels, logic would suggest that there is a correlation. However, chronic nicotine use does not seem to modify the GABAergic or dopaminergic systems in the nucleus accumbens, thus suggesting that while locomotor activity does increase due to dopaminergic activity, it is not related to chronic use[31] (Figure 3.4).

There is evidence, though, that there are some dose-related neurotransmitter and neuroendocrine effects which are related to plasma nicotine levels. For example, studies show that NE and epinephrine levels rise along with the increased availability of arginine vasopressin, B-endorphin, adrenocorticotropic hormone, and cortisol. Since these are important behaviorally active neurochemicals, cognitive states and neurobiological responsivity are altered for extended periods of time. Pharmacological effects of nicotine coupled with an almost instantaneous delivery system—inhalation—are what provokes powerful biological and psychological effects.

Conversely, other nicotine delivery systems (i.e., the patch or the gum) do not produce the same levels of reward. This particular effect—the relationship between the neurobiological effects of nicotine, external stimulus, and plasma levels—also indicates areas for treatment study, especially with the consideration of behavioral modification techniques.[29]

Not all of the neurobiological effects of nicotine, however, are understood in relationship to the level of dose or amount of cigarettes smoked. For example, there are studies that indicate smoking increases beta-endorphin levels that are usually associated with rewarding activities like nursing or rebound during stress.

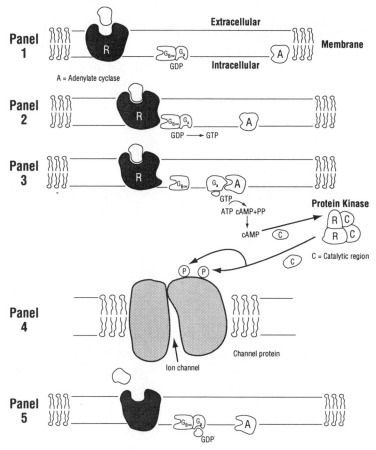

FIGURE 3.4. G-Protein Pharmacology

SOURCE: S. P. Salloway. "Dopamine Receptors in the Human Brain." *Psychiatric Times*, 1994;11(5):28.

However there are reports that plasma neuromodulator increases are commonly seen in smokers without "subjective stress." Host factors, what the user brings to the drug challenge, are important differences among patients in both **"constitution and/or physiological dependence and are likely to contribute to variations in physiological response to nicotine."**

Smoking may produce BE release in some individuals under certain circumstances. In others, in combination with psychological stress, smoking may enhance the likelihood of BE release, since smoking and stress may produce additive or synergistic effects. Effects may also be accentuated during and immediately after puberty.

Comorbidity and Cholinergic Effects

Smoking and drinking have always seemed to go together—or at least, they both seem to be widely consumed and abused substances, often in combination. It is clear that they both contain similar psychopharmacological properties which may be at the root of their simultaneous use. In addition, studies show that these two substances may actually enhance the effects of each other by stimulating locomotor activity (LMA) and DA turnover.

There is some evidence that the cholinergic pathways may be involved in this activity. ACh's neurotransmitter functions indicate that they may be involved in numerous activities involving the senses, including taste, pain, and feelings of warmth or cold. In fact, some of the effects of ACh may be hormonal in nature, rather than simply neurotransmission. ACh receptors are both muscarinic and nicotinic. Until recently, the muscarinic receptors were well understood, whereas the nicotinic receptors were unclear. At this time, it is now clear that there are numerous nicotinic receptors that serve multiple functions. For example, there is evidence that the development of both myasthenia gravis and Alzheimer's disease is related to the function of the ACh receptors.

In regard to the comorbid use of alcohol and tobacco, there is also evidence that the combined use of these two substances increase DA and NA release. Nicotine's NA effects are also mediated by activation of nicotinic ACh receptors. It is this activity that would appear to effect LMA, which is induced by alcohol and mediated by nicotine. Recent studies show change on the basis of levels of alcohol use, which in turn, may be affected by levels of alcohol used.[32]

"Additive effects of stress and nicotine have been reported for peripheral cortisol in humans and for peripheral corticosterone, epinephrine, and glucose in animals. Stress-dependent effects of nicotine are also reported for EEG activity."[33]

There is, of course, evidence that gender and racial characteristics may alter responses to nicotine and tobacco use.[29]

One of nicotine's most important neurobiological effects is its ability to act as either an antagonist or agonist, thus explaining some of its seeming paradoxical behavioral effects. Uniquely, nicotine provokes a certain level of nAChR desensitization, which is linked to its antagonist effects and may explain why the behavioral effects vary from smoker to smoker. Further, specific receptor site desensitization may also explain why tolerance and dependence vary from individual to individual. This "conditioned" response—receptor site desensitization—may theoretically be linked to treatment resistance and relapse.[27–29]

Action as an agonist also occurs at nAChR sites which receive Ca^{++} into the receptors, which would seem to account for nicotine's ability to affect behavior or create dependence.[27–9] There is some evidence that at this point, after Ca^{++} or other ions are absorbed, the receptor's sensitivity is altered and further action transfer is prevented.[27–9] This "desensitization" property is what then changes the effects of nicotine from agonistic to antagonistic.

Nicotine's Neurobiological Link to Tolerance and Dependence

It would seem that nicotine's unique sensitization properties for specific nAChRs is also related to nicotine tolerance. Studies show that smokers whose central nAChrs become desensitized quickly are more likely to increase their tobacco use as opposed to those whose receptors have a longer desensitization period.

Nicotine's ability to provoke acetylcholine-like effects at specific receptor sites is also largely responsible for another secondary effect, which is the release of other mood-regulatory neurotransmitters such as dopamine or serotonin. Likely sites of such release include the nucleus accumbens, the substantia nigra, the raphe nuclei, the hippocampus, and the reticular formation. Therefore, depending on the specific neuronal bonding, nicotine's action channel effects are a result of its provoking acetylcholine. Ultimately, the level of nicotine in the neurological system is at the root of its behavioral effects.[27]

Studies with male mice repeatedly dosed intravenously with nicotine do, however, show that high tolerance levels will be present without changes in neuroreceptor sites. These studies theorize that corticosterone release caused by the repeated nicotine injections may be the cause of the behavioral changes and tolerance of nicotine in mice. Why this occurs remains unclear at this time, although environmental effects that are due to the repeated injections may be the source of conditioning which provokes further effects in the hippocampal-hypothalamic-pituitary-adrenal axis.[34,35]

While it's clear that nicotine's neurobiological effects are similar to those of most drugs of abuse, especially the opiates, there are significant differences. As most opium addicts have discovered, smoking is the quickest delivery system to the brain, and tobacco smoking, which is rarely self-limiting, works in a most efficient manner. However, unlike most drugs of abuse, tobacco does not create the same crippling psychological effects, which we see with other addictive drugs, due to self-limits by the smoker, who senses—or self-titrates—to a level necessary to achieve a system-wide balance of alternatives without tachycardia or panic.

What is also unique about tobacco is that its harmful side effects—the extraordinary biological damage from carbon monoxide and other chemicals released in smoke—are not, for the most part, related to the pharmacological effects of nicotine or the biological reward–reinforcement drives that fuel use. Unlike that of other drugs of abuse, nicotine's damage is primarily a by-product of its delivery system, not necessarily the drug itself. In fact, tobacco causes a self-imposed maintenance system—not unlike methadone. This may be one reason to use the "patch" continuously for recidivism.

There is, however, considerable evidence that the drive to smoke is also related to environmental cues that tip off a neurobiological response, which is a pattern of behavior in other drug use. For example, there are data that seem to indicate that the taste and smell of burning tobacco can become so powerful that they directly cue the tobacco use levels. Once they light up, cigarette smokers seem to know how many cigarettes they need and how long they need to smoke to get the effect they seek.

This would seem to indicate that neurobiological research should not only focus on the dependency and addiction aspects of smoking but look closely at how environmental stimuli provoke a drug-seeking neurological response. We believe that the biological model for nicotine addiction is close to that of both opiates and stimulants. However, nicotine's reward–reinforcement abilities are not as apparent as those of cocaine or crack, which is another reason that it's not minimized by experts and not viewed primarily as a "drug."[28]

One final question remains: Is there a genetic or biological predisposition to cigarette smoking or a significant biological difference among smokers themselves? We have alcohol-preferring and nonpreferring rats and Schukit's studies in humans. What about nicotine-preferring animals or people?

"Chipping" is a well-recognized phenomenon among approximately 5%–10% of all smokers.[36] Chippers are smokers who use fewer than five cigarettes a day. Unlike other smokers, who tend to self-regulate their biological response to tobacco through the type and strength of the cigarette and frequency of use, chippers do not self-regulate. They do not seem to have a biological need to adjust their blood nicotine levels. Instead, they report that their smoking behavior is related directly to emotional needs.

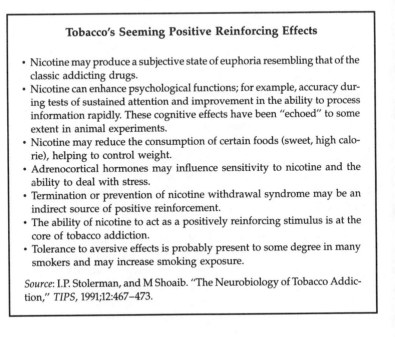

Tobacco's Seeming Positive Reinforcing Effects

- Nicotine may produce a subjective state of euphoria resembling that of the classic addicting drugs.
- Nicotine can enhance psychological functions; for example, accuracy during tests of sustained attention and improvement in the ability to process information rapidly. These cognitive effects have been "echoed" to some extent in animal experiments.
- Nicotine may reduce the consumption of certain foods (sweet, high calorie), helping to control weight.
- Adrenocortical hormones may influence sensitivity to nicotine and the ability to deal with stress.
- Termination or prevention of nicotine withdrawal syndrome may be an indirect source of positive reinforcement.
- The ability of nicotine to act as a positively reinforcing stimulus is at the core of tobacco addiction.
- Tolerance to aversive effects is probably present to some degree in many smokers and may increase smoking exposure.

Source: I.P. Stolerman, and M Shoaib. "The Neurobiology of Tobacco Addiction," *TIPS*, 1991;12:467–473.

Data show that chippers, generally, can stop smoking when they want to and suffer fewer adverse effects when they do stop.

Because tobacco use among chippers (22%) can vary—some will smoke a pack or more a day[37] and then cut back easily—it may be that chippers have different tolerance levels. Or they may not respond as others do to repeated use. One type of smoker may be sensitive to and may have diminished acute tolerance for both aversion and reward. If such an individual experiences increased aversive effects and smokes infrequently, his or her smoking pattern may mimic that of the chipper.[27]

Russell suggests that there are differences in the basic types of smokers: "peek seekers," who attempt to absorb as much nicotine as possible and "trough maintainers,"[38] who actually absorb less nicotine from each cigarette.

Rosecrans and Karan have suggested "that either up- and/or down-regulation of nAChR may be associated with conditioned response and the development of nicotine dependence and that chronic tolerance of the up-regulation of nAChR may be a prerequisite for physical withdrawal."[27]

Further evidence that there may be a biological predisposition to the effects of nicotine is found in the examination of other drug-sensitive populations. Shuckit and Gold[39] reported that children of alcoholics (COAs) who were predisposed to alcohol dependence had higher tolerance levels to alcohol than non-COAs, probably due to desensitization. While the COAs were able to use higher levels of alcohol without intoxication or impairment, they ultimately developed a higher degree of tolerance and dependence.

This process may be the same for tobacco smokers. Dependent smokers are the ones who are initially more sensitive to nicotine and may be born with or acquire increased pleasure–reward from nicotine. Persons prone to nicotine addiction would be more able to use this drug than others to stimulate or relax themselves.

Other theories suggest that tolerance developed over long periods of time results from a drive to provoke reward or reinforcement and that it is the time this takes in each individual that predetermines addictive probability.[40]

Collins, Minor, and Marks[41] report that animal studies (mice) tend to confirm that genetics are clearly involved in tobacco dependence. Data demonstrate that different strains of mice displayed different tolerance and sensitivity levels to tobacco challenges.[41]

Although this is discussed in depth in Chapter 5, there are significant data that demonstrate that depressed smokers use more tobacco and have more difficulty stopping than others.[40] Rosecrans and Karan report that certain predisposed individuals will smoke simply to relieve stress, without realizing that their drive to smoke is a result of nicotine's ability to provoke Da or 5-HT and the resultant effect on reward and arousal systems in the nucleus accumbens or other neurological systems.[27]

In the long run, the many similarities will outweigh the differences between the neurobiological effects of tobacco use and other substance abuse. Neuroscientific research will lead to new theories of how drugs affect brain reward circuits and how host and drug factors lead to addiction liability. While the dopaminergic system and other neurotransmitters may ultimately control nicotine's reward–reinforcement effect, the basic difference may lie in the cultural and the environmental factors that drive use. Tobacco is, after all, one of the most frequently used drugs, without euphoric or withdrawal-based impairment. Thus, regular (many-times-a-day) self-stimulation can be almost unlimited. Tobacco use is also a function of conditioning and a response to external stimuli. The classic smoking "clichés"—after meals or sex, or when working, or when relaxing in front of the TV—are actually conditioned responses that put the smoker in a vicious circle or auto-pilot response. Once desensitization occurs, there may be a greater neurobiological drive among tobacco users than among all other drug takers to continue to seek nicotine's perceived reward.[27]

Conclusion

The various drugs of abuse—opiates, stimulants, alcohol, nicotine, cannabinoids, cocaine—have distinct and apparently different primary sites of neurotransmitter action. They directly interact with different receptors or other cell-surface proteins. Therefore, if the addictive effects of drugs of abuse are mediated via a common final pathway with similar net chronic effects, it is likely that post-receptor intracellular targets are involved.[42] With continued understanding of the cellular basis for drug reward and the possibility that drug and other rewards are separable, new pharmacological treatments which focus on the positive aspects of the drug-taking experience and reduce drug reward and drug taking may be possible. The natural history of addiction is as a chronic, relapsing disorder. Treatments which focus on the reduction of the likelihood of relapse after detoxification may redefine the neurobiology of addiction, and may lead to a new understanding of the persistence of drug-taking and new treatments.

References

1. Helzer J, Burnam A. Epidemiology of alcohol addiction: United States. In Miller NS, ed. *Comprehensive Handbook of Drug and Alcohol Addiction*, Chap. 1. New York: Marcel Dekker, 1991.

2. Miller NS, Gold MS. Familial and genetic evidence for common transmission of drug or alcohol addiction (in press).

3. Gardner EL, Lowinson JH. Marijuana's interaction with brain reward systems: Update 1991. *Pharmacol Biochem Behav.* 1991;40:571–580.

4. Wise RA, Rompre PP. Brain dopamine and reward. *Ann Rev Psychol.* 1989;40:181–225.

5. Wise RA. Action of drugs of abuse on brain reward systems. *Pharmacol Biochem Behav.* 1980;13(Suppl. 1):213–223.

6. Wise RA. The neurobiology of craving: Implications for the understanding and treatment of addiction. *J Abnorm Psychol.* 1988;97(2):118–132.

7. Miller NS, Gold MS. The relationship of addiction, tolerance, and dependence to alcohol and drugs: A neurochemical approach. *J Substance Abuse Treat.* 1987;4:197–207.

8. Stolerman IP, Shoaib M. The neurobiology of tobacco addiction. *Trends Pharmacol Sci.* 1991;12:467–473.

9. Chen J, Paredes W, Li J et al. In vivo brain microdialysis studies of delta9-tetrahydrocannabinol on presynaptic dopamine efflux in nucleus accumbens of the Lewis rat. *Soc Neurosci Abstr.* 1989;15:1096.

10. Kosten TR. Neurobiology of abused drugs: Opioids and stimulants. *J Nerv Ment Disease.* 1990;178(4):217–227.

11. Rasmussen KI, Aghajanian GK. Withdrawal-induced activation of locus coeruleus neurons in opiate-dependent rats: Attenuation by lesions of the nucleus paragigantocellularis. *Brain Res.* 1989;505:346–350.

12. Rasmussen K, Fuller RW, Stockton ME et al. NMDA receptor antagonists suppress behaviors but no norepinephrine turnover or locus coeruleus unit activity induced by opiate withdrawal. *Eur J Pharmacol*. 1991;197:9–16.

13. Hughes JR, Higgins ST, Bickel WK. Nicotine withdrawal vs. other drug withdrawal syndromes: Similarities and dissimilarities. *Addiction*. (submitted).

14. Hughes JR. The nicotine withdrawal syndrome: A brief review and update. *Int J Smoking Cessation*. 1992;1:21–26.

15. Hughes JR. Protracted withdrawal. *Am J Psychiatr*. 1994;151:785–786.

16. Strahlendorf JC, Strahlendorf HK. Response of locus coeruleus neurons to direct application of ethanol. *Neurosci Abstr*. 1984;7:312.

17. Baumgartner GR, Rowen RC. Clonidine vs. chlordiazepoxide in the management of acute alcohol withdrawal syndrome. *Arch Int Med*. 1987;147:1223–1226.

18. Gold MS. *The Good News About Drugs and Alcohol*. New York: Villard Books, 1991.

19. Verbanck P, Seutin V, Massotte L et al. Yohimbine can induce ethanol tolerance in an in vitro preparation on rat locus coeruleus. *Alcoholism: Clin Exper Res*. 1991;15(6):1036–1039.

20. Satel SL, Price LH, Palumbo JM et al. Clinical phenomenology and neurobiology of cocaine abstinence: a prospective inpatient study. *Am J Psychiatr*. 1991;148:1712–1716.

21. Gold MS, Dackis CA. New insights and treatments: Narcotics and cocaine addiction. *Clin Therapeutics*. 1985;7(1):6–21.

22. Dackis CA, Gold MS. Psychopharmacology of cocaine. *Psych Annals*. 1988;18(9):528–530.

23. Bozarth MA, Wise RA. Anatomically distinct opiate receptor fields mediate reward and physical dependence. *Science*. 1984;224:516–517.

24. O'Brien CP. Conditioned responses, craving, relapse and addiction: An interview with Charles P. O'Brien. *The University of Florida Facts about Drugs and Alcohol Newsletter*. 1992;4:1.

25. Jarvik ME, Schneider NA. Nicotine. In Lowinson JH, Ruiz P, Millman RB, Langrod J, eds. *Substance Abuse: Comprehensive Textbook*. Baltimore: Williams & Wilkins, 1992.

26. Langley JN, Dickinson WL. On the local paralysis of peripheral ganglia, and on the connection of different classes of nerve fibers with them. *Proc R Soc*. 1989;46:423–431.

27. Rosecrans JA, Karan LD. Neurobehavioral mechanisms of nicotine

action: Role in the initiation and maintenance of tobacco dependence. *J Substance Abuse Treatment*. 1993;10:161–170.

28. Stolerman IP, Shoaib M. The neurobiology of tobacco addiction. *Trends Pharmacol Sci*. 1991;12:467–473.

29. Pomerleau OV. Nicotine and the central nervous system: Biobehavioral effects of cigarette smoking. *Am J Med*. 1992;93(Suppl. 1A): 1A-2S–1A-7S.

30. Damaj MI, Martin BR. Is the dopaminergic system involved in the central effects of nicotine in mice? *Psychopharmacology*. 1993;111: 106–108.

31. Fund YK, Lau YS. Chronic effects of nicotine on mesolimbic dopaminergic system in rats. *Pharmacol Biochem Behav*. 1991;41:57–63.

32. Blomqvist O, Soderpalm B, Engel J. Ethanol-induced locomotor activity: Involvement of central nicotinic acetylcholine receptors? *Brain Res Bull*. 1992;(29):173–178.

33. Gilbert DG, Meliska CJ, Williams CL et al. Subjective correlates of cigarette-smoking-induced elevations of peripheral beta-endorphin and cortisol. *Psychopharmacology*. 1992;106:275–281.

34. Grun EA, Pauly JR, Collins AC. Adrenalectomy reverses chronic injection-induced tolerance to nicotine. *Psychopharmacology*. 1992; 109:299–304.

35. Matta SG, Fosteer CA, Sharp BM. Nicotine stimulates the expression of cFos protein in the parvocellular paraventricular nucleus and brainstem catecholaminergic regions. *Endocrinology*. 1993;132(5):2149–2156.

36. McKennel AC, Thomas RK. *Adults' and Adolescents' Smoking Habits and Attitudes*. London: British Ministry of Health, 1967.

37. Shiffman S. Tobacco "chippers"—individual differences in tobacco dependence. *Psychopharmacology*. 1989;97:539–547.

38. Russel MAH, Feyerabend C. Cigarette smoking: A dependence on high-nicotine boli. *Drug Metab Rev*. 1976;8:29–57.

39. Schuckit MA, Gold EO. A simultaneous evaluation of multiple markers of ethanol/placebo challenges in sons of alcoholics and controls. *Arch Gen Psychiatr*. 1988;45:211–216.

40. Pomerleau DS, Pomerleau OF. The effects of a psychological stressor on cigarette smoking and subsequent behavioral and physiological responses. *Psychophysiology*. 1987;24:278–285.

41. Collins AC, Minor LC, Marks MJ. Genetic influences on acute responses to nicotine and nicotine tolerance in the mouse. *Pharmacol Biochem Behav*. 1988;30:269–278.

42. Bhat RT, Baraban JM. Activation of transcription factor genes in striatum by cocaine: Role of both serotonin and dopamine systems. *J Pharmacol Exp Therap.* 1993;267:496–505.

Additional Sources

Grenhooff J, Svensson TH. Nicotinic and muscarinic components of rat brain dopamine synthesis stimulation induced by physostigmine. *Arch Pharmacol.* 1992;346:395–398.

Vezina P, Blanc G, Glowinski J et al. Nicotine and morphine differentially activate brain dopamine in prefrontocortical and subcortical terminal fields: Effects of acute and repeated injections. *J Pharmacol Exp Therapeut.* 1992;261(2):484–490.

4

Tobacco and the Body

With each investigation of tobacco use, the question always arises: Why would anyone still smoke? Smoking is not a survival or essential behavior. Smoking is, without any question, neurobiologically and psychologically addicting. It is socially unacceptable and becoming more so. As "users" of tobacco, smokers find themselves an ostracized minority, like current cocaine, marijuana, or heroin users.

Perhaps one answer to this paradox lies in the user's "denial," an aspect of addiction common to all legal and illegal substance abuse that is described in greater detail in Chapter 5. Denial can prevent cocaine users from recognizing that their business and financial lives are jeopardized by their continued use or can prevent alcoholics from admitting that drinking is endangering themselves and others.

Smokers are even more vulnerable to denial because this form of addiction does not produce the euphoria and "rush" that stimulants create, or the somnambulance, dysphoria, hallucinations, and loss of coordination that stimulants or opiates produce.

But, more important, the biological damage—cancer, heart disease, strokes and other diseases that accompany tobacco use—

Tobacco's U.S. Toll

Every day, 375 Americans die from smoking-related cancer and 700 from smoking-related heart and lung disease.

Up to 25% of pregnant women smoke: 4600 infant deaths, 14% of preterm deliveries, and up to 30% of low-birth-weight babies are attributed to smoking.

Each day, 3000 teenagers become regular smokers; the average starting age is 13 for cigarettes and 10 for smokeless tobacco.

Source: From Morain, Claudia. "Smoking Gun." *American Medical News*, July 19, 1993. Statistics from American Academy of Pediatrics, Centers for Disease Control, Environmental Protection Agency, Surgeon General.

---

does not appear for years after use begins. Since most people start using cigarettes in their late teens and early adult years, a time of "psychological invulnerability," and there is some evidence that it can *increase* perceived attentiveness and reduce stress or fatigue, its grip becomes even tighter over time.

The Pharmacology of Cigarettes

Cigarettes, whether they are "tall," "slim," "filtered," or "unfiltered," are basically delivery systems for approximately 10 milligrams of nicotine, of which about 1%–2% reaches the lungs. Once it hits the small airways and alveoli, the nicotine easily crosses the blood–brain barrier and is on its way. Some nicotine may enter the system through the buccal mucosa, and alkaline pH is usually present in that case. But the lungs and brain are only two of the many targets affected by nicotine and tobacco smoke by-products. In fact, nicotine is absorbed throughout the body. Microscopic particles of tar circulate throughout the body seeking sites such as the liver, where it is converted into cotinine and nicotine-N-oxide in an approximately 90:10 ratio. The site of absorption is also somewhat mediated by the pH level of the smoke. Most cigarettes have a pH of around 5.5, which is rapidly ionized; therefore, it is not usually absorbed orally.

Any unmetabolized nicotine remains in the system, stimulating neurotransmitters and mediating the addictive effects of the drug. The rapidity of absorption and the subsequent rate of excretion provoke cravings and tolerance.[1]

Once the nicotine is absorbed, the cardiovascular system is stimulated through ganglionic effect. In high doses, dizziness, nausea, and vomiting may be present, which dissipate after the body adjusts. With a half-life of 2–4 hours, nicotine remains active in the user for 6–8 hours, especially with a "regular recharge" with every additional cigarette. In effect, nicotine stimulates the user around the clock, not just with each new dose. Once on its way to the brain, it's also metabolized quickly. The liver and kidneys absorb it and then excrete the remaining nicotine, with anywhere from 2%–35% eliminated through the urine.[1]

Nicotine is also a centrally acting stimulant with many diverse neurological effects (see Chapter 3). As any first-time smoker will recall, the experience was probably accompanied by dizziness or nausea, a phenomenon also seen in chronic users who smoke frequently and inhale deeply. This, again, is an obvious reason why the euphoria theory of addiction is limited. Smoking behavior is reinforced, making smoking more likely with or without euphoria and despite negative first-dose effects. Smokers quickly become tolerant, and learn to control these negative feelings, in part, by changing how much and how deeply they inhale.

Several hormones, such as ACTH, prolactin, vasopressin, and growth hormone are released. The exact reason for this major hormonal reaction is not clear. However, some of the vertigo-like effects of nicotine are regulated by the release of the "chemoreceptor trigger zone" and chemoreceptors in the carotid body. Stress, whether perceived by the user or not, may underlie these hormonal reactions as they do for cocaine.[1]

The Effects of Smoking on Clinical Test Results

Cigarette smoking may cause increases in:
    Leukocyte counts
    Red cell mass
    Hemoglobin
    Carboxyhemoglobin
    Hematocrit
    Mean corpuscular volume
    Platelet aggregation
    Platelet adhesiveness
    Total serum cholesterol concentration
    Low-density lipoprotein levels
    Serum carcinoembryonic antigen levels
Cigarette smoking may cause decreases in:
    High-density lipoprotein levels
    Blood coagulation time
    Serum creatinine and albumin levels.

Source: Data from "Smoking and Health: A Report of the Surgeon General, 1979" In *Clinical Opportunities for Smoking Intervention: A Guide for the Busy Physician*. U.S. Department of Health and Human Services, Public Health Service, National Institutes of Health, 1986.

Mortality and Tobacco

According to the American Cancer Society's annual *Cancer Facts and Figures*, 46 million people in the United States were smokers in 1991 and almost 44 million had quit smoking cigarettes by 1991, "nearly half of all living adults who ever smoked." All of the people who continue to use cigarettes are putting themselves directly in the path of a fatal bullet.

Mortality rates directly or indirectly related to tobacco use correlate with length of use, although this varies from disorder to disorder. For example, smokers are more likely to develop lung cancer, but studies point out that there are more overall deaths due to cardiovascular disease. Thus the number of people who die due to heart disease secondary to the effects of tobacco is greater. In fact, more than one-third of all cardiovascular deaths are related to smoking. Studies as far back as 1985 reported that 21% of cardiovascular disease and 19% of cerebrovascular stroke deaths were linked to smoking. Risks of aortic aneurysms, arterial thrombosis, hypertension, and peripheral vascular disease are also clearly increased by tobacco use.[1,2]

Since heart disease is the leading cause of death among men and lung cancer is now more prevalent among women than cancer of the breast, reduction in smoking patterns still has a long way to go. In addition, smokers have at least a 2:1 increased chance of developing cancer at nonpulmonary sites.[2]

Smoking-Associated Illnesses

Why or how nicotine or smoking leads to a number of serious and often fatal diseases is well studied although not definitively agreed upon. It is reasonably clear that a by-product of cigarette smoke, carbon monoxide, does increase the risk of cardiovascular disease. The amine compounds are widely thought to be carcinogens and, along with other toxic by-products of smoke, are clearly a cause of premature aging.[2]

However, cardiovascular disease and lung cancer are hardly the only diseases in the smoking-and-mortality top 10. Add to those laryngeal cancer, atherosclerotic peripheral vascular disease, chronic obstructive pulmonary disease, chronic bronchitis, oral and esophageal cancers, fetal growth retardation and low birth weight, possible links to other cancers (e.g., bladder, pancreas, kidney, intestinal), and respiratory infections in both smokers and those who are exposed to secondary smoke.[1]

Smoking and the Heart

Nicotine's effects on the cardiovascular system are well documented, causing increased heart rate and blood pressure. The increase in metabolic response to nicotine may cause coronary artery spasm and an increase in coronary blood flow.[2] A smoker has a 30%–45% greater chance of developing a coronary disorder than a nonsmoker. In fact, smoking is the single most important risk factor a person can change to slow the development of heart disease. If a person stops smoking, within a year, her or his risk factors for coronary heart disease (CHD) will decrease by 50% and revert to baseline in another 24–36 months. In fact, short-term smoking reduction of one to three days can even alleviate cardiovascular stress.[3,4] Several reports indicate that the return to baseline heart rates can be permanent, once smoking has ceased. However, other studies indicate that heart rate may not return to normal in certain individuals. The nicotine effect on heart rate, according to Persico, "suggests that while heart rate adaptation to nicotine is largely of an acute nature, there also may be a chronic component. Its role, though usually minor, should become detectable in a few subjects, because of wide interindividual variability."[5]

Other studies have reported that by cessation of smoking, men can almost completely reduce their risk of a first myocardial infarction within five years and, depending on smoking levels, within two–three years for females. These data seem to carry over to those over 65, whose mortality rate from heart attack seems to be "significantly less" than that of those who continue to smoke. Similarly, rates of atherosclerosis are reduced, while sense of smell and taste are increased in the nonsmoking aged population.[2]

Smoking's cardiovascular effects are often compared to those of other common stimulants such as caffeine or the illicit drug cocaine. One study compared smoking a cigarette and drinking a cup of coffee on the basis of pre/post puffing and pre/post consumption changes. Changes in heart rate, which rose, were similar both pre and post puffing and drinking. However, there were observations of the anticipatory effects of lighting, puffing, and smoking on both motor function and EEG data, which may indicate that there is an unconscious cardiovascular stimulation associated with the neurobiological drive caused by the perceived need to smoke.[6]

Respiratory Effects

Respiratory disorders, apart from lung cancer and obstructive pulmonary disease, are particularly virulent among smokers. There is an increased risk of emphysema, pulmonary tuberculosis, influenza, pneumonia, bacterial bronchitis, lung dysfunction resulting from decreased α_1-antitrypsin, silicosis, asbestosis, and other lung disorders that result from workplace dangers.[2]

The mechanism of destruction is not entirely understood; however, it is thought that nicotine, inhaled through tobacco smoke, utilizes catecholamines to affect lipids, which in turn contribute to coronary artery disease. Most likely, LDL (low-density lipoprotein) levels rise and HDL (high-density lipoproteins) levels drop. Further, smoking causes platelet activity to increase, which decreases or inhibits prostacyclin, which in turn causes greater blood coagulation. Other cardiac effects are also linked to catecholamine stimulation. For example, cardiac arrhythmias may be linked to high levels of carbon dioxide, which is a by-product of inhaling burning tobacco smoke. (Not incidentally, this same combination—combustion and CO_2—causes fatality in fire fighters, plane crash victims, and those caught in house fires.) Carbon monoxide and nicotine produced by tobacco smoke also have a cause-and-effect relationship in other cardiovascular disorders.

Cancer

Can nicotine itself be linked to cancer? The answer is still unclear. There is some evidence that nicotine does become a carcinogenic compound known as nitrosonornicotine, yet no one has demonstrated that it is produced in sufficient levels to be damaging.

The links between cancer and smoking are clearly related to by-product compounds such as tar and nicotine-derived nitrosamines.[1,2] As far as lung cancer is concerned, however, it's believed that nicotine stimulates leukocytes, which stimulate certain pancreatic enzymes that harm the alveoli in the lungs.[1]

Regardless of the direct mechanism, lung cancer is the leading cancer killer, with 153,000 deaths projected in the United States in 1994. Men who smoke are 22 times more likely to develop lung cancer. Women are 12 times more likely. While 87% of all lung cancer cases are smoking-related, cancer of the mouth, pharynx, esophagus, cervix, bladder, kidney, and pancreas are also related to tobacco use. Smokers have a greater risk of stroke—about two times as high—which is even higher among women using oral contraceptives.[7] Smokers, depending on age, are also at high risk of developing leukemias, although the exact mechanism involved is not yet clear.[8]

As with heart disease, the risk of lung cancer can be reversed once smoking stops. In fact, after five years, the risk diminishes by 40% and may be totally reversed in 15 years.[4] Smoking cessation also reduces the risk of developing a second, smoking-related cancer.[9] Similar data exist in studies of risk of other cancers, such as pancreatic cancer, which may also be reversed after 10–15 years.[2]

Not surprisingly, patients who continue to smoke, even though they are undergoing radiation treatments for head and neck cancer, have a reduced chance of recovery.[10]

Smoking and Pregnancy

Smoking and pregnancy are, obviously, a dangerous combination, but again, the psychological blanket of denial and the physiological addiction caused by nicotine make it difficult to convince many women that even reduced levels of tobacco intake are harmful. In spite of the fact that smoking has been linked to spontaneous abortion, vaginal bleeding, reduced blood flow to the fetus, and a variety of pre- and postnatal abnormalities,[2] still, according to a phone survey conducted by the Office on Smoking and Health of the Centers for Disease Control (CDC) in 1991, about one in five pregnant women smoked during pregnancy.[11]

In the larger scheme of things, cigarette smoking may actually be more harmful to the unborn child than any illegal drug, even cocaine. Once inhaled, gases produced by tobacco smoke, such as carbon monoxide, can cause placental hypoxia, decreasing the delivery of vital nutrients to the fetus. Nicotine seems to prevent acetylcholine-facilitated amino acid transport and disrupts the activities of the cholinergic receptor.[2]

This theory, that tobacco is more dangerous than cocaine, is shared by many experts and is based on studies that show that nicotine can affect a particular set of cholinergic receptors that are involved in acetylcholine neurotransmission during the latter third of pregnancy. An animal model, using rats, determined that when exposed to one-half to one pack of cigarettes a day, rats were born with significantly fewer of these nerve cells.

"It's as though nicotine equals cocaine plus this additional effect," according to Theodore Slotkin, Ph.D., professor of pharmacology at Duke School of Medicine. Slotkin also notes that virtually all the deleterious effects of cocaine—SIDS, low birth weight, learning disabilities, and so on—are the same problems encountered by cigarette users. And not surprisingly, he also indicates that the vast percentage of crack users and other substance abusers smoke.

Some experts feel that the effects of cocaine on birth weight and head circumference are not significant but become significant when the user is a smoker.[11] According to Ira Chasnoff, M.D., president of the National Association for Perinatal Addiction Research and Education, most people underplay the dangers of tobacco during pregnancy: "If you look at the sheer numbers and the impact on general health, tobacco by far is a bigger player."[11]

Not surprisingly, children exposed to passive smoke are far more likely to have pulmonary disorders, including bronchitis, pneumonia, tracheitis, and ear infections.[2] Adults who live with a smoker have a risk of getting lung cancer much greater than if they had worked in an environment of open asbestos for decades. Studies have also shown increases in the occurrence of nasal cancer, brain tumors, asthma, and breast cancer in passive smokers.[2]

Smoking, Aging, and Alzheimer's Disease

If smoking is hazardous to the neurobiological and physiological functions of adults and children, then logic would also dictate that it is far worse for the geriatric population. *Surprisingly, the answer is yes and possibly no.* Clearly smoking is one, if not the number one, risk factor for cardiovascular disorders and multiple cancers among the elderly. However, there are some reports that smoking has some relationship to prevention of Parkinson's disease, endometrial cancer, and preeclampsia among the elderly. Numerous epidemiological reports suggest that the antiestrogen effect of smoking may be related to a reduced risk of endometrial cancer in this population.[1,12] Smokers, especially elderly white men and women, have lower bone mineral density in the hip area, so that reduced smoking or quitting entirely may be a factor in preventing fractures in the elderly.[13]

Most intriguing is the reported effect on Alzheimer's Disease (AD) which afflicts 60%–70% of all dementia patients. Significant among AD patient symptoms are perceptual and visual problems. In addition, postmortem studies of AD patients have indicated a significant deficit in nicotinic receptor sites in the neocortex and hippocampus compared to the normal population.[13,14] Studies report that when nicotine is injected subcutaneously,[12] it has reduced attention deficits and increased reactive and perceptual abilities; however, it has not improved the major problems associated with AD: the inability to process visual and sound images that affect memory.[14]

The basis for occurrence may lie in nicotine's cholinergic agonist effects and its ability to raise acetylcholine levels. It's thought that the collapse of the forebrain's cholinergic systems may be at the root of AD effects. Therefore, increased levels of nicotine may increase cholinergic levels and reduce cognitive dysfunction, both post- and presynaptically.

However, there still are many questions raised about this hypothesis since there has been a wide range of results within the AD populations studied. And the results have been inconsistent, affecting only certain cognitive functions.[14] In addition, many of the study populations vary in education levels and concomitant health-related problems (e.g., hypertension) all of which seem to have some sort of unexplained relationship to the effects of nicotine on AD.[12]

All of the above leads to the conclusion that there are some promising results among AD patients who are treated with some form of nicotine (e.g., gum or a patch); however, this does not suggest that smoking among the elderly should, in any way, be encouraged.[12] Since these studies do not indicate that nicotine can enhance the AD patient's lifestyle or daily living patterns, more studies on the effect of increased cholinergic activity may also be appropriate. It may be that safer, less dependency-building medications may be developed that can perform this function and bring some relief of this tragic disorder.

Smoking and Weight

Among patients who are deep in denial regarding the health hazards of smoking, the leading excuse to continue is related in one way or another to weight. Virtually everyone who has given up smoking has experienced some sort of weight gain, and most firmly believe that smoking suppresses appetite. Is this the case?

On the surface, it would appear that cigarettes do have an anorectic effect, and studies of both humans and mice indicate that it does reduce desire for certain types of foods, such as sweets. This is consistent with nicotine's neurobiological effect related to the release of catecholamines, specifically norepinephrine and serotonin. Therefore, the repeated stimulation of the brain's satiety center or a direct metabolic level effect may be linked to smoking's reputation as a weight reduction tool.[1]

However, there is more to the issue of smoking and weight gain.

Contrary to what most people think, smokers actually seem to consume as much food as or even slightly more food than their non-smoking counterparts, and smoking does not appear to increase physical activity. Reduced caloric intake does not appear to be the reason that smokers seem to have and maintain a lower body weight. Studies indicate that weight reduction caused by nicotine is due to its effect on the metabolism of the smoker.[15] What occurs *in part* is similar to what occurs when most people try to lose weight: the rate of calories consumed is less than are expended due to the stimulating effects of nicotine on metabolic rate. (There do not appear to be major differences between males and females regarding smoking and weight gain or loss.)

When a person stops smoking, the resulting weight gain is usually minimal, most likely a result of increased desire for sweets—which now taste better—and no real cardiovascular or other health-related threat from weight gain occurs.[2] Our experience suggests that smokers do, for a limited time, eat more after they stop smoking, and then caloric intake is cut back once smoking resumes. Weight gain, for some, can be a big problem and troubling. Most weight gain takes place within the first two or three months after smoking is stopped, and the amount of weight gained is probably related to the level of smoking.[16] Weight gain may be a cardinal sign of nicotine abstinence.

This weight gain, however limited in some, is seen as a contributing factor in treatment resistant and relapsing smokers. Patients using nicotine gum, for example, report limited weight gain after cigarettes are discontinued. Frequently caffeine use, which often accompanies smoking, is also reduced because the change in metabolic rate no longer requires increased energy needs.[17]

There are, according to Perkins,[15] three possible reason why tobacco or nicotine is not, as widely considered, an anorectic agent:

1. Continued use of tobacco builds tolerance to the anorectic effects of nicotine.
2. The reward–reinforcement effect of smoking and eating at the same time becomes linked.
3. Smoking may affect the body's biological set point. Thus the body automatically controls its own weight gain or loss in relation to the level of smoking that occurs. (Once this set point is reached, it can be disrupted—by drugs or other environmental factors. The body continually adjusts to keep weight consistent. This theory—of set point and reset point—has been considered across the board in other substance abuse or drug use and appears to relate to nicotine effect in the same manner.

If nicotine is indeed responsible for reducing the set point, rather than affecting appetite or provoking anorexia, then eating habits will remain consistent even if smoking patterns change. The set point will remain fixed, at least for some time. However, once nicotine is withdrawn, it is likely that the set point will readjust along with increased feeding patterns. This process will change once again with smoking resumption, provoking a yo-yo pattern of weight loss and gain among smokers who try repeatedly to stop.[15]

Metabolism

Central to smoking's long-term effect on weight gain and loss are its overall effects on the user's metabolism. It's reasonably certain that nicotine acutely provokes sympathoadrenal activity and, as mentioned above, encourages release of neurotransmitters, including NE, DA, 5-HT, hormones, and peptides like cortisol and neuropeptide Y, all acting to increase metabolic activity. In addition, the effects of the myriad of chemical compounds in smoke, especially carbon monoxide, cyanide, and tar, along with "puffing" rates and other smoking-related behavior, can affect metabolism. For example, continued "overpuffing" may simulate or stimulate panic attacks. Other activity, such as eating and smoking, may also combine to create differing biochemical states that affect metabolism, all related to smoking behavior.[18]

Among smokers, as in nonsmokers, RMR (resting metabolic rate) accounts for over three-quarters of all energy dispensed. Therefore, even a minimal jump in energy use could change weight and metabolic balance. Although, in general, it has been shown that the acute effects of nicotine intake are minimal, they can be significant, especially when linked to increased physical activity or eating.[18]

Some other studies suggest that fluid intake may have an impact on weight changes among smokers.[16] Studies of users of nicotine gum suggest that increased volume of gum may also decrease weight in both current and former smokers.[16] There is also some evidence that increased tolerance levels lead to less weight reduction.[16]

It's clear that smoking's involvement in weight gain and loss is linked somewhat to reduced caloric intake, but it is more likely to be controlled by the effects of metabolic changes, brain-mediated micronutrient preferences and resultant eating patterns, and other environmental factors that increase energy expenditures.

Secondhand Smoke

One of the most controversial aspects of smoking is its secondary effects. Virtually no one who smokes will admit to this phenomenon, and virtually all people who do *not* smoke do not want to tolerate smoking in their "space." They have good reason.

The EPA calls secondhand smoke a "Class A Carcinogen." It attributes over 3000 deaths each year to secondhand smoke along with 300,000 cases of infant respiratory infection, and 6,000 new cases and 1 million exacerbated cases of asthma in children. Shockingly, one to three adults who smoke expose almost nine million children to secondhand smoke at home.[19] Secondary smoke is, in fact, much more of a risk for cardiovascular deaths than a cancer risk, resulting in 35,000 unnecessary deaths per year.[4,19,20] According to a study by Stanton A. Glantz and Dr. William Parmley, secondhand cigarette smoke killed 37,000 Americans a year due to heart disease, 3700 due to lung cancer, and 12,000 due to other cancers. Further, links to lung cancer in nonsmokers and secondhand cigarette smoke have been reported by the Surgeon General's office.[20]

Several studies with laboratory animals conclude that secondhand smoke leads to an accumulation of fat in the arteries, which, in turn, is the link to passive smoking and cardiovascular disorders. Other studies show that platelet levels are also affected, contributing to increased risk of blood clots within the arteries.[4]

Reversibility of Effects

Finally, for smokers, even those who are in denial, there is good news. Most mortal effects linked to tobacco are in patients who have smoked for decades, and since there is a clear relationship between dose duration and effect in tobacco, its deadly effects can be reversed once smoking stops. Of course, as in all cumulative dose-related disorders related to tobacco, the ratio of reversibility to damage is linked to time smoked versus time stopped.[1,2]

References

1. Jarvik ME, Schneider NG. Nicotine. In Lowinson JH, Ruiz P, Millman RB, Langrod J, eds., *Substance Abuse: Comprehensive Textbook*. Baltimore: Williams & Wilkins, 1992.
2. Lee EW, D'Alonzo DO. Cigarette smoking, nicotine addiction, and its pharmacologic treatment. *Arch Intern Med*. 1993;153:34–48.
3. Rosenberg L, Palmer JR, Shapiro S. Decline in the risk of myocardial

infarction among women who stop smoking. *N Engl J Med.* 1990; 322:213–217.

4. Dewar MA. Smoking cessation. *Am Fam Physician.* 1990;41:1191–1194.

5. Persico AM. Persistent decrease in heart rate after smoking cessation: a 1-year follow-up study. *Psychopharmacology.* 1992;106:397–400.

6. Hasenfratz M, Jacober A, Battig K. Smoking-related subjective and physiological changes: Pre- to postpuff and pre-postcigarette. *Pharmacol Biochem Behav.* 1993;46:527–543.

7. Gunby, P. Legal challenge to medically correct smoking bans. *JAMA.* 1994;271(8):577.

8. Sandler DP et al. Cigarette smoking and risk of acute leukemia: Associations with morphology and cytogenetic abnormalities in bone marrow. *J Nat Cancer Inst.* 1993;85:1994–2003.

9. Richardson GE et al. Smoking cessation after successful treatment of small-cell lung cancer is associated with fewer smoking-related secondary primary cancers. *Ann Intern Med.* 1993;119:383–390.

10. Browman GP et al. Influence of cigarette smoking on the efficacy of radiation therapy in head and neck cancer. *N Engl J Med.* 1993;328: 159–163.

11. Cotton, P. Smoking cigarettes may do developing fetus more harm than ingesting cocaine, some experts say. *JAMA.* 1994;271(8):576–577.

12. Brenner DE, Kukull WA, van Belle G et al. Relationship between cigarette smoking and Alzheimer's disease in a population-based case-control study. *Neurology.* 1993;43:293–300.

13. Hollenbach KA et al. Cigarette smoking and bone mineral density in older men and women. *Am J Public Health.* 1993;83:1265–1270.

14. Jones GM, Sahakian BJ, Levy R et al. Effects of acute subcutaneous nicotine on attention, information processing and short-term memory in Alzheimer's disease. *Psychopharmacology.* 1992;108:485–494.

15. Perkins KA. Effects of tobacco smoking on caloric intake. *Br J Addiction.* 1992;87:193–205.

16. Nicotine Dependence, Congressional Office of Technology Assessment, 1994 Report to 103rd Congress of the United States. 1994:224.

17. Schwid SR. Nicotine effects on body weight: a regulatory perspective. *Am J Clin Nutr.* 1992;55:878–884.

18. Perkins KA, Epstein LH, Sexton JE. Effects of nicotine on hunger and eating in male and female smokers. *Psychopharmacology.* 1992;106:53–59.

19. Morain, C. Smoking gun. *Am Med News.* July 19, 1993.

20. Study shows how secondhand smoke hurts heart. *New York Times,* November 22, 1992.

5

The Psychiatric Aspects
of Tobacco Use

How closely do the psychiatric effects of tobacco use match those of cocaine users, marijuana smokers, and opiate addicts? There are multiple answers to this question, and the answers, to some extent, frame the ever-widening national debate surrounding tobacco use and the addictive effects of nicotine.

When exploring the psychiatric effects of nicotine, it is important to remember that the tobacco industry has fought, both in the media and in the pages of scientific journals, the concept that tobacco is a drug or that nicotine is dangerous. The industry totally and completely asserts that tobacco use is something like drinking a beverage and not dangerous or addictive. In April 1994, the nation was witness to one of the most extraordinary examples of this position when each of the chief executive officers of the five largest cigarette manufacturers stood up before a congressional committee and declared that, in their view, "nicotine is not addictive."

This public declaration by executives of companies whose economic clout substantially influences the American economy was one of the most defining moments of the public debate about the harm that tobacco can do to everyone, especially the country's youth. On one side are the forces of science that have developed thousands of indisputable studies revealing physiological damage caused by smoking that have resulted in the banishment of tobacco advertising from the public airways and turned smokers into an outcast minority. On the other side is an extraordinarily powerful industrial and economic lobby that has been able to almost entirely ignore the scientific evidence and defeat almost all legal challenges while promoting itself through media images that are as well known by children as are Disney characters.[1]

The tobacco lobby has not simply stonewalled. It has produced its own version of the "scientific evidence" about tobacco, which is designed to minimize the psychiatric and psychological aspects of tobacco use. The basic position is that the product is "safe"; therefore, the industry has only to justify "why" people should and can continue to use it.

How the Tobacco Industry Lives with Itself

The tobacco industry has sponsored a considerable amount of research into its "product safety," some of which has been published in respected journals. These studies not only provide the tobacco industry's scientific justification but also reveal exactly how it views tobacco from a psychosocial point of view. One study is particularly revealing.[2]

The industry poses the same question that has baffled anyone who understands the devastating effects of tobacco: Why do people smoke?

The answer it proposes, however, is quite different from those of other scientific investigators. The tobacco industry agrees that people smoke for both the pharmacological and nonpharmacological reasons that other researchers have reported—but with an entirely different effect.

The industry's studies agree that peripheral stimulation is one pharmacological effect. However, that first cigarette of the day is not induced by craving or dependence, according to these industrial researchers, but rather by a simple desire for a "jump start." Their studies show that most people who smoke indicate that "increased mental alertness produced by smoking/nicotine is an important aspect of their smoking motivation."[2]

Along with this rationale, industry-sponsored studies report that even more people say that smoking has only an anxiolytic effect. In other words, after that first smoke of the day gets them going, the cigarette becomes invaluable in the face of everyday stress. Whether a person smokes within the first 30 minutes of awakening is generally considered the nicotine dependence question and, if yes, a poor prognostic sign.

"We believe," Robinson and Pritchard report, "that a more reasonable hypothesis concerning why people smoke is that smokers use cigarettes primarily as a 'tool' or 'resource' that provides them with needed psychological benefits (increased mental alertness; anxiety reduction, coping with stress)."[2] Other studies,[3] suggest that over 80% of those studies see "pleasurable relaxation" as a key benefit people derive from smoking.

The data presented by the industry-sponsored studies, however, do raise one of the key questions—known as the *nicotine paradox*—that has to be examined in determining smoking's psychological aspects. Do people smoke *only* for mental stimulation or for mental relaxation? Yes, the tobacco industry says, tobacco's effects are really that benign. In fact, they say, the 1988 Surgeon General's Report was incorrect. Nicotine found in tobacco leaves is *not* like cocaine derived from the coca leaf; instead, it is more like the relatively benign effects of caffeine as described by the Surgeon General in a 1964 report.

Tobacco isn't dangerous, industry-sponsored studies say. In fact, it is actually a "resource" tool that people can depend upon when "common sense" tells them they need a little stimulation. This rationale allows the industry to state that smoking is not addicting; rather, it is "habituating." The entire question of addiction is rarely addressed as a result. Nicotine is simply lumped into a relatively safe category along with theophylline in tea, theobromine found in cocoa, and caffeine in everything from diet soda to coffee. Industry executives readily admit that nicotine is psychoactive but insist that a cigarette in the morning is no more indicative of addiction than the 10 A.M. coffee break. It does not, they repeatedly point out, result in either intoxication or extreme withdrawal symptoms, both essential elements of an addictive substance.

One industry sponsored study states:

> In our opinion, it is political zeal rather than scientific merit that supports the conclusion of the 1988 SGR that the "pharmacologic and behavioral processes that determine tobacco addiction are similar to those that determine addiction to drugs such as heroin and cocaine.
>
> We believe that Warburton[4] has developed a balanced, functional theory of nicotine use that recognizes the beneficial psychological effects of nicotine. This "resource," or "psychological tool" hypothesis holds that people smoke cigarettes primarily for purposes of enjoyment, performance enhancement and/or anxiety reduction. This theory also passes the common-sense test of why people smoke. They smoke, not because they are addicted to nicotine, but because they achieve some benefits from smoking, enjoy these benefits which are totally compatible with everyday tasks and stresses, and choose to continue to enjoy these benefits.

The concomitant biological damage that this "resource" leads to is never mentioned.[2]

The Real Truth Behind Tobacco's Psychiatric Effect

No matter what the merits of the tobacco industry's case for the safety and "benefits" of smoking are, one fact is clear; thus far, it has worked. It has kept tobacco from being classified as a dangerous drug and has prevented any real controls on its use or distribution.

One reason is that most smokers do believe that intoxication and euphoria are the signs of a drug with dependence potential. Addicting drugs change behavior: the sloppy drunk, the heroin addict slumped over in a corner, immobilized, or the cocaine addict, overenergized and talking a mile a minute. Tobacco use has an entirely different image. Thus, it is not addicting. This is, however, incorrect. Addictive drugs are actually used differently by different populations under a wide variety of circumstances. Compulsive use is not seen in all groups with all drugs. In fact, one widely overlooked reason why people continue to take drugs that cause unpleasant reactions after tolerance and dependence develop is not *only* because they seek reward, but also because they seek a return to "normal."

Another important claim of industry-sponsored studies is that the reported nonpharmacological aspects of use are not as important as the widely studied pharmacological aspects of smoking. Further, the industry relies on self-reported use studies, which frequently result in suspect data.[5]

The best way to approach the arguments that are put forth to defend smoking's psychological impact is to examine its use in situations where the issues of "relaxation" or "stimulation" have no real relevance. Tobacco's real psychiatric impairment is best understood by examining use patterns among those who are the victims of its biological and neurological effects.

Comorbidity and Tobacco

Perhaps no other data speak to the psychiatric issues outlined in the box and involving smoking than these:

- The Centers for Disease Control report that only 3% of the 20 million smokers in the United States who try to quit each year are successful.[6]

Addiction is. . .

Defined by the presence of

- Drug seeking behaviors
- Compulsive use of the drug(s)
- Relapse
- Denial of the consequences of use

Considered a disease based upon

- Genetic studies
- Common neurotransmitter neuroanatomy
- Common psychosocial treatments
- Common biological treatments

- Among smokers who have lost a lung to cancer or undergone major cardiovascular surgery, about 50% continue to smoke.[6]
- In a 1991 Gallup Poll, 70% of current smokers reported that they considered themselves "addicted" to cigarettes.[6]
- NIDA's 1985 National Household Survey on Drug Abuse (NHSDA) showed that 84% of 12- through 17-year-olds who smoked one pack or more of cigarettes per day felt that they "needed" or were "dependent" on cigarettes.[6]
- The NHSDA data show that young smokers develop tolerance and dependence, increase the amount they smoke, and are unable to abstain from nicotine. These findings suggest that the addictive processes in adolescents are fundamentally the same as those studied in adults.[6]
- Several studies have found nicotine to be as addictive as heroin, cocaine, or alcohol.[6]

Another important fact that is overlooked by those defending cigarette use is that far more people are actually addicted to tobacco than are addicted to other drugs simply on the basis of daily (or even hourly) exposure to nicotine. And the issue is not legality or access. For example, fewer than 10% of those who consume alcohol are considered alcohol dependent, *but approximately 85%–90% of cigarette smokers smoke at least five cigarettes every day.*[7–10] Only 2%–3% of smokers (or about 7%–10% of those who try quitting) stop smoking for one year, and most daily smokers report that they feel dependent on smoking and have experienced withdrawal symptoms.[6,11–13]

Is There a Biological Link?

Does smoking correlate with other psychiatric disorders beyond addiction levels? Are those who suffer from psychiatric disorders more likely to smoke? Is there a biological link to smoking and mental illness?

Seemingly so. Studies indicate that 56% of patients with schizophrenia and 41% of those with affective disorders smoked. In fact, 52% of the entire sample were smokers, which is a far higher percentage than the rest of the adult population (25%–30%). This and other studies also show a positive association between smoking and tardive dyskinesia.[14] Other studies have shown that up to 88% of schizophrenics smoke, and almost half of all anxiety and personality disorder patients are smokers. Anxiety levels are also associated with tobacco use and with relapse.[15]

Smoking, Depression, and Alcohol

There are also significant studies that clearly demonstrate a relationship between smoking and depression and also data that indicate that giving up tobacco is a much more difficult task for the depressed patient than for the rest of the population. This relationship—smoking and depression—has been widely ignored by the media and, of course, industry studies.

Do people who suffer from a psychiatric disorder alleviate

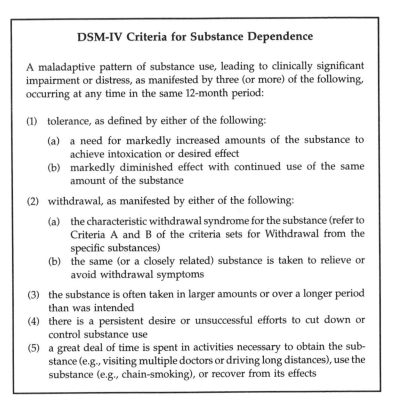

DSM-IV Criteria for Substance Dependence

A maladaptive pattern of substance use, leading to clinically significant impairment or distress, as manifested by three (or more) of the following, occurring at any time in the same 12-month period:

(1) tolerance, as defined by either of the following:

   (a) a need for markedly increased amounts of the substance to achieve intoxication or desired effect
   (b) markedly diminished effect with continued use of the same amount of the substance

(2) withdrawal, as manifested by either of the following:

   (a) the characteristic withdrawal syndrome for the substance (refer to Criteria A and B of the criteria sets for Withdrawal from the specific substances)
   (b) the same (or a closely related) substance is taken to relieve or avoid withdrawal symptoms

(3) the substance is often taken in larger amounts or over a longer period than was intended
(4) there is a persistent desire or unsuccessful efforts to cut down or control substance use
(5) a great deal of time is spent in activities necessary to obtain the substance (e.g., visiting multiple doctors or driving long distances), use the substance (e.g., chain-smoking), or recover from its effects

their psychiatric symptoms by smoking? Do they smoke to ease the side effects of their medication? Do they now smoke because they are addicted? Are these people biologically predisposed to smoke?[14] Getting the answers to these questions and others can become a complex task. For example, research studies of smokers who are in an abstinence mode may observe physiological changes—weight increase, EEG, and heart rate changes—along with psychological symptoms such as restlessness, insomnia, and irritability that can mimic or mask true psychiatric symptoms. Further, tobacco can exacerbate the effects of several psychiatric

(6) important social, occupational, or recreational activities are given up or reduced because of substance use

(7) the substance use is continued despite knowledge of having a persistent or recurrent physical or psychological problem that is likely to have been caused or exacerbated by the substance (e.g., current cocaine use despite recognition of cocaine-induced depression, or continued drinking despite recognition that an ulcer was made worse by alcohol consumption)

Specify if:

With Physiological Dependence: evidence of tolerance or withdrawal (i.e., either Item 1 or 2 is present)

Without Physiological Dependence: no evidence of tolerance or withdrawal (i.e., neither Item 1 nor 2 is present)

Course specifiers

Early Full Remission
Early Partial Remission
Sustained Full Remission
Sustained Partial Remission
On Agonist Therapy
In a Controlled Environment

Source: Adapted with permission from *Diagnostic and Statistical Manual of Mental Disorders*, Fourth Edition. Copyright 1994 by the American Psychiatric Association.

medications (haloperidol and amitriptyline). In addition, blood levels of drugs drawn from those in a smoke-free inpatient program may be significantly different from blood levels found in outpatients who have not ceased smoking.[16] It's often difficult to examine the relationship between smoking and other psychiatric disorders simply because so many victims of mental health problems are smokers. Often, people suffering from heart disorders, for example, are depressed, and frequently they are smokers. Where does this relationship begin and where does it end? How widespread is this seeming connection?

Substance Abuse

Features

The essential feature of Substance Abuse is a maladaptive pattern of substance use manifested by recurrent and significant adverse consequences related to the repeated use of substances. There may be repeated failure to fulfill major role obligations, repeated use in situations in which it is physically hazardous, multiple legal problems, and recurrent social and interpersonal problems (Criterion A). These problems must occur recurrently during the same 12-month period. Unlike the criteria for Substance Dependence, the criteria for Substance Abuse do not include tolerance, withdrawal, or a pattern of compulsive use and instead include only the harmful consequences of repeated use. A diagnosis of Substance Abuse is preempted by the diagnosis of Substance Dependence if the individual's pattern of substance use has ever met the criteria for Dependence for that class of substances (Criterion B). Although a diagnosis of Substance Abuse is more likely in individuals who have only recently started taking the substance, some continue to have substance-related adverse social consequences over a long period of time without developing evidence of Substance Dependence. The category of Substance Abuse does not apply to caffeine and nicotine.

The individual may repeatedly demonstrate intoxication or other substance-related symptoms when expected to fulfill major role obligations at work, school, or home (Criterion A1). There may be repeated absences or poor work performance related to recurrent hangovers. A student might have substance-related absences, suspensions, or expulsions from school. While intoxicated, the individual may neglect children or household duties. The person may repeatedly be intoxicated in situations that are physically hazardous (e.g., while driving a car, operating machinery, or engaging in risky recreational behavior such as swimming or rock climbing) (Criterion A2). There may be recurrent substance-related legal problems (e.g., arrests

---

Some of the data are well recognized:

Out of 10 alcoholics, 8 are smokers, and studies show that the more they drink, the more they smoke. Smoking can be a relapse cue or trigger in alcoholics and vice versa.[13]

Smokers often try to stop smoking but may be unable to

for disorderly conduct, assault and battery, driving under the influence) (Criterion A3). The person may continue to use the substance despite a history of undesirable persistent or recurrent social or interpersonal consequences (e.g., marital difficulties or divorce, verbal or physical fights) (Criterion A4).

CRITERIA FOR SUBSTANCE ABUSE

A. A maladaptive pattern of substance use leading to clinically significant impairment or distress, as manifested by one (or more) of the following, occurring within a 12-month period:

(1) recurrent substance use resulting in a failure to fulfill major role obligations at work, school, or home (e.g., repeated absences or poor work performance related to substance use; substance-related absences, suspensions, or expulsions from school; neglect of children or household)

(2) recurrent substance use in situations in which it is physically hazardous (e.g., driving an automobile or operating a machine when impaired by substance use)

(3) recurrent substance-related legal problems (e.g., arrests for substance-related disorderly conduct)

(4) continued substance use despite having persistent or recurrent social or interpersonal problems caused or exacerbated by the effects of the substance (e.g., arguments with spouse about consequences of intoxication, physical fights)

B. The symptoms have never met the criteria for Substance Dependence for this class of substance.

Source: Adapted with permission from *Diagnostic and Statistical Manual of Mental Disorders*, Fourth Edition, Copyright 1994 by the American Psychiatric Association.

because of a psychiatric problem. A study conducted in 1985 reported that 65% of those who tried to stop smoking had also had a previous bout with depression.[18] Other studies confirm that smokers with major depression are more likely to have failed in their attempts to stop smoking. These studies show the greater likelihood of those who "ever smoked" (76%) to be depressed than of those who had never smoked (52%). This 2:1 ratio was confirmed by other studies.[19]

The issue of smoking and depression centers on the question of common biological vulnerability versus self-medication. Since there is a higher rate of use among those with a history of depression, does this indicate that they are more likely to continue smoking to ward off nicotine withdrawal symptoms (i.e., depression), or is depression linked to smoking in some other, genetic manner?

There is speculation that adolescent use is prompted by the desire to ward off symptoms of depression or anxiety. This self-treatment method may expose genetically vulnerable people to tobacco at an age when smoking patterns are initiated, thus beginning a chicken-and-egg pattern.

Other studies show that cigarette smoking may be associated more strongly with symptoms of depression rather than with depression itself[18] and that the "degree" of dependence on tobacco is also related to the likelihood of depression.

One study found that smokers who had previous bouts of depression were also likely to become more addicted to nicotine and similarly that those who had smoked for a lengthy period were also likely to become depressed.[19] Data from Kenneth S. Kendler, M.D., a specialist in psychiatric–genetic linkage confirms these findings, especially among heavy (more than a pack a day) smokers. In additional studies of fraternal and identical twins, he noted the same results.[19]

These studies of genetic links confirm theories that certain personality types may be more vulnerable to tobacco addiction. These studies suggest that children who suffer from anxiety, restlessness, rebelliousness, aggression, extroversion, and depressive symptoms will more than likely be smokers as adults.

Alcohol and depression, as noted above, are also closely linked to smoking. According to Dr. John R. Hughes, a psychiatrist at the University of Vermont School of Medicine, "There is probably a gene that influences behavior that then leads to alcohol abuse." The same is most likely true of smoking, he says. With the decline of smokers, "We're weeding out smokers who aren't so dependent," says Dr. Hughes. "Smoking becomes a better marker for psychopathology."[19]

Dr. Naomi Breslau, an epidemiologist, has also examined the links between smoking, anxiety disorders, and depression. Breslau conducted several studies, including one study of one thousand 21- to 30-year-olds, that revealed "a strong connection between smoking, anxiety and depression." "I was surprised," Dr. Breslau reported. "You didn't think of smokers as sick people exactly."[19]

Among her other findings were that common withdrawal symptoms from tobacco use, including irritability, nervousness, and dysphoria, were more severe in those with a history of depression than in the rest of the population who quit smoking. In fact, when measured for age, marital status, education, or socioeconomic level, there was no difference among populations. Other reports suggest that in this group of smokers who had previously experienced depression, the withdrawal symptoms were more severe and pronounced. With the exception of decreased heart rate, abstinent smokers reported symptoms matching DSM-III-R nicotine withdrawal criteria more frequently than any other symptoms.[20]

These studies also indicate that those with a history of anxiety disorders—not those who were drug- or alcohol-dependent—suffered more severe withdrawal symptoms. Other studies of young adults in the Detroit area[20] confirmed these results and also indicated that a history of smoking and depression was likely to result in continued smoking. Interestingly, a history of anxiety disorders, as defined by DSM-III-R, did not correlate with increased likelihood of continued smoking.[20]

The evidence above would seem to indicate and reconfirm the theory that smokers with a history of major depression and other affective disorders are less likely to become abstinent. The reason for this phenomenon is, according to Dr. Breslau, "the greater positive reinforcing effects of smoking, chiefly, mood elevation and arousal, rather than the reinforcing effects of nicotine on the relief of withdrawal discomfort. To date, there is no empirical evidence bearing on this hypothesis, which clearly merits examination in future research.[20]

There are other intriguing clues to the link between smoking and depression. For example, it's well known that reduced smoking rates have been significant only in well-educated populations. Smoking levels among blue-collar workers and high school dropouts have remained level for three decades, a phenomenon most likely linked to social factors. For example, there may be less peer pressure among less-educated populations to quit.

However, if this theory is true, then why are there still middle-class college graduates with heavy smoking patterns? There are two potential answers: a genetic link or a comorbid psychiatric problem.

In an interview in the *New York Times*, Dr. "Sandy" Glassman says that smoking should be regarded as a distress signal: "Say your office is on Park Ave. and your patients are bankers and lawyers. Well, so many of these people have quit that if someone comes in and tells you they're a smoker, you can look at that person with a jaundiced eye, saying that if it's a woman there's a big chance that she has depression, and if it's a man there's a good chance that he's an alcoholic."[19]

Other experts, such as Kendler, have postulated that the relationship between smoking and depression is not causal; rather, they are both the product of a biological predisposition. Others agree, like Breslau, who says, "My suspicion is that there are certain personality characteristics that are closely linked to the nervous system, to the underlying neurophysiology of the individual."[20] Jack E. Henningfield of NIDA suggests that sociological factors create a "spectrum of vulnerability" to a range of addictions, including cocaine and nicotine.[7]

Smoking and Other Psychiatric Problems

Smokers today are under extraordinary pressure from the medical profession, family, friends and co-workers to stop. If they haven't, they may be at high risk for a range of psychiatric illness, which suggests that a new group of "dependent patients" may be appearing in physicians' offices. It's critical that they be correctly diagnosed and referred for further treatment. General practice physicians and psychiatrists will have to work closely together in light of the fact that depression and smoking are hardly the only concomitant mental health problem facing smokers.[12]

Studies of the Epidemiologic Catchment Area (ECA) data in St. Louis also revealed the correlation between smoking and other common psychiatric problems.

Not surprisingly, the largest "ever smoked" group was alcoholics. Depression, however, ranked second. Those who had "ever smoked" appeared in greater numbers than the rest of the population among agoraphobics, dysthymics, and panic disorder victims. In fact, alcoholics accounted for 25% of the population of smokers. All too frequently, treatment remains a one-problem-at-a-time process. In general, this has been true of the treatment of alcoholics. It is vitally important to help the alcoholic stop smoking immediately, since it does appear that many can be successful in stopping alcohol before they die of smoking-related problems. Ironically, AA's founders, Bill Wilson and Dr. Bob, both stopped drinking but died of emphysema and oral pharyngeal cancer, respectively.

Rates of nicotine addiction are also far higher than in the rest of the population among those with anxiety disorder alone (two times higher), anxiety and depression (three times higher), and smokers with concomitant problems (four times higher). There clearly is some sort of association between smoking and anxiety disorders, but this does not seem to be a factor in the patient's ability to stop, as it is in depressed groups. Since smokers claim that cigarettes have an anxiolytic effect, it's likely that this cohort would report high levels of use.[18]

Other psychiatric diagnoses have been associated with smoking. For example, there seems to be a high correlation between smoking behavior and schizophrenia.[17] Some data[22] suggest that as many as three-quarters of all schizophrenics are smokers, which is almost three times the national average.[18] Other data report that between 80% and 90% of all hospitalized schizophrenics are smokers, with men at the higher end of the scale.

This link with schizophrenia is very likely due to nicotine's dopaminergic effects in the nucleus accumbens and the prefrontal cortex, which lead to the reward–reinforcement response common among smokers. There is evidence of hypoactivity in the prefrontal cortex that suggests an association between this activity and schizophrenia. Therefore, the suspected link between nicotine and the negative aspects of schizophrenia may occur in this system.[18]

Reinforcement and Cues

In seeking to understand tobacco's psychiatric effect, it is important to recognize its role as a "reinforcing agent," which is part of the "nicotine paradox" raised by tobacco industry studies. Any drug that fits into this category is usually defined by the lengths a person is willing to go to obtain it—sacrificing eating, sex, work, family, and so on. Included in this equation are the environmental aspects that surround the drug's use—availability, quantity, concomitant use—and even the personal history of the drug user.

Measured against other drugs (cocaine, stimulants, opiates) that produce a reward, tobacco certainly meets these criteria for many users. Studies of smokers who were abstinent overnight[18] demonstrated a clear increase in the reinforcement level of tobacco by measuring the level and intensity of puffing. Not surprisingly, similar behavior is found in those similarly deprived of food in other studies.

The strong, often overwhelming, reinforcing values of tobacco can also be seen in the response to "cues" that are thought to provoke desire in nonabstinent smokers. Something as remote as a cigarette smoked across the room or even seeing a person light up on TV or in a movie, may provoke the desire to smoke. Unfortunately, there are no reliable or controlled studies that confirm these anecdotal observations.[23]

Perkins and co-workers suggest that other environmental factors such as gender, length of abstinence, and the self-initiated "schedule" that smokers put themselves in have an impact on the reinforcing value of tobacco. In the case of gender, it has been observed that women may be more "sensitive" to nicotine than men. In addition to gender, genetic factors or preferences may play an important role.

When observing the reinforcing effects of tobacco, it is necessary to look at overall use patterns. For example, if one is without access to tobacco but observes a variety of "cues," it is likely that one will devote more energy to obtaining tobacco and also garner a greater reward when finally obtaining it. Other data suggest that the "schedule" of reinforcement impacts on nicotine-seeking behavior, and the way the schedules are constructed by users may change their pattern of use significantly.[23]

Cognitive Effects and Anxiety

One of the underlying forces behind tobacco's reinforcing value is its cognitive effect. There is some evidence according to studies among two populations—students and athletes—that nicotinic response does affect cognitive performance, increased alertness, and reduced anxiety.

A 1992 study demonstrated that tobacco use prior to exams was not actually related to reduction of anxiety but that students were seeking increased alertness. The study's authors speculate that the anxiolytic effects of smoking are "limited to acute, short-term stressors," and that the preexam use was simply a method of reinforcing the level of attention desired. These results lead to the conclusion that anxiolytic effects of cigarettes are most effective in controlling "more immediate stressors, such as an argument or receipt of bad news . . . thus it may be that individuals with a greater predisposition to anxiety become regular smokers and that smoking helps them deal with acute stressors; sedative smoking primarily relieves withdrawal symptoms of irritability and anxiety; smoking does not act positively to combat external stressors in the person's life, but rather controls withdrawal symptoms which result from interruption of chronic nicotine administration."[24]

It is possible that increased smoking levels before exams is due to an unsubstantiated belief—a myth that smoking will help them prepare for exams—that's used by smokers to justify continued use in spite of well-known consequences.[20]

The data above may correlate with the belief that nicotine use can enhance performance in other arenas, for example, among athletes.

While cigarette smoking has diminished, use of smokeless tobacco (ST) has increased. Surprisingly, ST use has actually increased at a rate of 11% since 1974, primarily among athletes. ST use seems to be de rigueur among professional baseball and football players, who believe that it stimulates salivary activity, improves their reactive capabilities, and contributes to the attentive state necessary to perform well.[25]

Some studies confirm this belief with measures of arousal coming between 4 and 12 minutes after ST consumption. There are widespread anecdotal reports from athletes that reinforce the belief that ST quickens reaction time and focal abilities.

Recent studies report that nicotine has a positive effect on "vigilance, rapid information processing, state dependent learning, and retention of paired associates" along with stress reduction.[21] Studies of animal models tend to confirm the anecdotal report that nicotine enhances "cognitive efficiency in both speed and accuracy of information processing."[25] These reports, not surprisingly, tend to correlate with other reports of nicotine's "paradoxical" effects.[25–27]

There are also some selected studies that indicate that nicotine has a positive effect on memory not only through enhancement of attention and focus but directly. There is some evidence that nicotine can assist the user in the formation of associations, not just enable more effective mnemonic processing. In one study smokers were able to improve recall of forgotten information after nicotine input indicating that postlearning memory may be affected by nicotine input.[28]

Animal studies at Duke University and other sites are now examining whether use of a nicotine patch can enhance memory and attentiveness. This gives rise to the question of whether or not nicotine patches will become more commonplace in the future.[29]

Along with the questions that surround nicotine's effects on memory are additional questions that suggest a significant effect on mood. It is known that nicotine does affect stress levels under certain circumstances. But does this translate into mood elevation? It is clear that some of nicotine's stimulating effects are dose-related; however, it is unclear whether this is a perceived effect. To date, there are many conflicting studies, some of which indicate that nicotine's motor reflex inhibitory capabilities may alleviate stress and thus elevate mood. But stress itself produces many reflex actions (e.g., nail biting) designed to prevent anxiety and control mood. Among the results of the many conflicting studies of nicotine's effect on mood is the suggestion that smoking's effect on mood may actually be attributed to the relief of withdrawal rather than a specific mood-elevating result.[11]

Craving

One of the most complicated psychological behaviors surrounding smoking is what is commonly referred to as *cigarette craving*. Some smokers complain of cravings for months while others complain of craving and a "white knuckle" abstinence struggle lasting a year or more after quitting. Studies suggest that craving may be the result of a multitude of factors that affect each smoker differently on different occasions.

The biological and neurological effects of tobacco have led to the study of cravings as a response by the smoker to the perceived beneficial effects of smoking and the perceived negative effects of withdrawal. However, because the level of craving varies so

widely, it is hard to suggest that the perceived physiological stimulation from smoking is the cause of cravings. In fact, it is likely
that there are also numerous factors such as the perceived psychological benefits that combine to cause craving.[30]

Are cravings universal? Once smoking stops, cravings, either
due to nicotine deficit or simply from a behavioral perspective,
occur in about two-thirds of all smokers. Frequently, the change in
"ritual" is enough to provoke this phenomenon and it is a contributing factor in relapse. Some studies have reported that former
smokers who used nicotine gum found it effective in reducing
nicotine loss but not cigarette cravings.[15,30]

While further study is needed, it is clear that a variety of
factors combine to provoke cravings. However, the most important factor is the individual smoker's view that cigarettes some-
how provide some sort of benefit. Until that psychological reference point can be reversed, craving remains a constant threat to
abstinence. As each former smoker learns to replace the cigarette
in times of stress or at other key moments, then the power of
cravings will diminish.[31] (Methods for continued abstinence in the
face of cravings are discussed in Chapter 7.)

Other Effects

Among the other psychological effects of tobacco is its impact
on specific senses, especially taste and smell. Several studies have
explored the behavioral cues produced by the smell of burning
tobacco and the taste of different tobacco blends, which suggest
that smokers do adjust their "puffing" habits when taste is altered
by tar concentration. These studies suggest that "tar yield" is the
desired goal rather than nicotine volume.

Other studies[32] have explored the relationship between burning tobacco and the conditioned response it may cause.[28] There is
evidence that the thousands of chemicals that are by-products of
burning tobacco and the nicotine load do create "a conditioned

association between the sensory aspects of smoking and the pharmacological effects of nicotine."[32] These studies[33,34] also report that the "throat scratching stimulus" caused by cigarette smoke may become a behavioral component of the reward drive associated with smoking.[35]

Chronic and Acute Tolerance

Nicotine's addictive potential is well documented. Does it, however, produce the tolerance and subsequent dependence and withdrawal that are almost always present in other drugs of abuse?

In the classic sense, nicotine does produce tolerance since there is evidence that, to some degree, each cigarette smoked during the day produces a slightly lower response. However, this response may be mostly subjective in nature, not biological. On the other hand, there is also evidence that the presence of tolerance in smokers may be from a "short-term change" in sensitivity at the receptor sites affected by nicotine. This tends to help reinforce the conclusion seen in other psychological aspects of smoking: Smokers may be driven differently from both a biological and psychological point of view.[36]

If smoking does create tolerance, does it follow that all smokers become nicotine-dependent? From an epidemiological standpoint, it would seem that most are. Most people smoke between one and two packs a day, and of that number, between 75% and 90% express a desire to quit. Still, most who try fail. The continued, compulsive use, in spite of well-known consequences, does suggest that smokers who don't stop are dependent.

The level of dependency, of course, is related to each individual's smoking patterns, and this is one reason why the tobacco lobby continues to claim that smoking is not addictive. There *are* "social smokers" who seem to reach for a cigarette at only selected times. There are others who "chip" and smoke only a few each

day, while the heaviest smokers, of four or five packs a day literally can't get out of bed without lighting up.

In the long run, however, the high relapse rates among abstinent smokers is the real clue to nicotine's dependency-producing
effect. If you smoke and can't stop, or if you smoke and stop
unsuccessfully, you are nicotine-dependent, just as if you were
dependent on cocaine or alcohol.[37]

Nicotine Withdrawal: Signs and Symptoms

Also contributing to the questions surrounding tobacco's
psychiatric effects is a long-term controversy surrounding its
withdrawal effects. For many decades, symptoms of withdrawal
from tobacco were either not recognized or were considered so
mild as to be unrelated to an addicted state. Some reports as far
back as the early 1940s suggested that withdrawal symptoms did
occur; however, there were no well-controlled studies at that time.
By the 1960s and 1970s, Larson, Haas, and Silvette[38–41] had documented withdrawal symptoms that suggested that tobacco withdrawal was not a function of "ritual behavior" but was due to
nicotine loss.

Studies of withdrawal symptoms, including irritability, anxiety, hunger, and cravings, were documented through placebo-
controlled studies utilizing nicotine gum. In these studies, symptoms were relieved with low-dose (2-mg) ad lib use of nicotine
polacrilex gum compared with the placebo. These studies—
suggesting a dose response effect of nicotine replacement's relief
of withdrawal symptoms—suggest that nicotine does provoke a
specific withdrawal syndrome.

Other studies have suggested that performance variables are
also affected by tobacco abstinence. This may be directly related to
biological levels of nicotine.[42] Snyder and Henningfield investi-
gated this phenomenon in a study examining nicotine gum versus
placebo and reported a dose response "reversal" of deficits in
speed of performance incurred with cessation of smoking."[38] This

result was confirmed by others, including Herning and Pick-worth, who administered nicotine gum during tobacco with-drawal to elicit a neurological response.[43]

How frequently do these symptoms occur, and how long will they remain? These are still open-ended questions. One study reports that significant withdrawal symptoms occur during the first week of cessation and subside after several days. However, irritability and anger may continue through the first month, and weight gain has been documented over two to three months.[44] One problem with all of these studies, however, is that many subjects succumb to the withdrawal syndrome and relapse. There is some evidence that nicotine replacement treatments during abstinence can relieve some of the withdrawal symptoms. How-ever, they do not relieve the behavioral aspects of smoking that also provoke relapse.

The following tables demonstrate that nicotine, one of the deadliest of all substances of abuse, is also one of the least tested agents of death.

By the late 1970s there were numerous studies establishing the validity of a nicotine withdrawal syndrome. Jarvik and his colleagues have produced a table of specific symptoms that in-clude information from several studies and the DSM-III-R.

Conclusion

The psychiatric aspects of smoking are the result of a complex series of neurological and behavioral events that stem from smok-ing's biological and ritualistic effects. There is a strong relationship between smoking and depression, alcoholism, and other psychi-atric illnesses. A history of these and other psychiatric disorders affects potential for cessation.[18]

In the long run, as more people stop smoking, there is a strong possibility that those who continue to smoke will be the most severely disabled and will require psychiatric evaluation and in-tensive, rather than a self-help treatment program. Already there

TABLE 5.1. Features of Various Drug Withdrawal Syndromes in Humans[a]

Features	Withdrawal syndrome[b]				
	Nicotine	Alcohol/sedative	Opioids	Amphetamine/cocaine	Caffeine
Pharmacological specificity	Y	Y	Y	Y	Y
Animal models	Y	Y	Y	Y	Y
Associated with tolerance	?	Y	Y	NT	Y
Precipitated withdrawal	N	NT	Y	NT	NT
Acute physical dependence	?	Y	Y	?	NT
Related dose and duration	?	Y	Y	NT	Y
Cross-dependence	NT	Y	Y	NT	NT
Symptom stages	NT	Y	Y	?	N
Gradual reduction decreases	Y	Y	Y	NT	NT
Protracted withdrawal	N	Y	Y	?	NT
Conditioned withdrawal	?	Y	Y	?	NT
Influenced by instructions	Y	Y	Y	NT	NT
Nonpharmacological tx effective	NT	Y	NT	NT	NT
Genetic effects	?	Y	NT	NT	NT
Neonatal withdrawal	N	?	Y	?	N

[a]References for table contents available upon request.
[b]N = no; Y = yes; NT = not tested.
Source: J. R. Hughes et al. Tobacco vs. Other Withdrawal. University of Vermont, Department of Psychiatry, 1994.

TABLE 5.2. Time Course for Acute Drug Withdrawal Syndromes

	Nicotine	Alcohol	Heroin	Caffeine	Cocaine
Onset	2–12 hrs	6–12 hrs	4–6 hrs	12–24 hrs	1 week
Peak	2–3 days	3–7 days	2–3 days	20–48 hrs	??
Duration	3–4 wks	1–2 wks	2 wks	5–7 days	Up to 10 wks

Source: J. R. Hughes et al. *Tobacco vs. Other Withdrawal*. University of Vermont, Department of Psychiatry, 1994.

TABLE 5.3. Among the Most Commonly Reported
Signs and Symptoms of Withdrawal

Mood changes	Hunger*
Irritability/frustration/anger*	Urges to smoke
Anxiety*	Craving*
Depression	Physiologic signs
Hostility	Weight gain*
Impatience	Decrease in heart rate*
Physiological symptoms	Increase in peripheral circulation
Drowsiness	Drop in urinary adrenalin, nora-
Fatigue	drenaline, cortisol
Restlessness*	Changes in EEG
Difficulty concentrating*	Changes in endocrine functions
Decreased alertness	Neurotransmitter changes
Lightheadedness	Performance deficits
Headaches	Sleep disturbance
Tightness in chest	Constipation
Bodily aches and pains	Sweating
Tingling sensation in limbs	Mouth ulcers
Stomach distress	Increased coughing

*Criteria for nicotine withdrawal taken from *Diagnostic and Statistical Manual of Mental Disorders*, Third Edition–Revised. Washington, DC: American Psychiatric Association, 1987.

Source: Jarvik M. E., Schneider N. G. Nicotine. In Lowinstein J. H., Ruiz P., Millman R. B., ed. *Substance Abuse: Comprehensive Textbook*. Williams & Wilkins, 1992.

DSM-IV: Nicotine-Related Disorders

Nicotine Dependence and Withdrawal can develop with use of all forms of tobacco (cigarettes, chewing tobacco, snuff, pipes, and cigars) and with prescription medications (nicotine gum and patch). The relative ability of these products to produce Dependence or to induce Withdrawal is associated with the rapidity characteristic of the route of administration (smoked over oral over transdermal) and the nicotine content of the product.

This section contains discussions specific to the Nicotine-Related Disorders. Texts and criteria sets have already been provided to define the generic aspects of Substance Dependence . . . that apply across all substances. Text specific to Nicotine Dependence is provided below. Nicotine intoxication and nicotine abuse are not included in DSM-IV; nicotine intoxication rarely occurs and has not been well studied, and nicotine abuse is not likely to be observed in the absence of Dependence. A specific text and criteria set for Nicotine Withdrawal is also provided below. Listed below are the Nicotine-Related Disorders.

Nicotine Use Disorder

305.10 Nicotine Dependence

Nicotine-Induced Disorder

292.0 Nicotine Withdrawal

292.9 Nicotine-Related Disorder Not Otherwise Specified

Nicotine Use Disorder

305.10　Nicotine Dependence

Also refer to the text and criteria for Substance Dependence. Some of the generic Dependence criteria do not appear to apply to nicotine, whereas others require further explanation. Tolerance to nicotine is manifested by the absence of nausea, dizziness, and other characteristic symptoms despite using substantial amounts of nicotine or a diminished effect observed with continued use of the same amount of nicotine-containing products. Cessation of nicotine use produces a well-defined withdrawal syndrome that is described below. Many individuals who use nicotine take nicotine to relieve or to avoid withdrawal symptoms when they wake up in the morning or after being in a situation where use is restricted (e.g., at work or on an airplane). Individuals who smoke and other individuals who use nicotine are likely to find that they use up their supply of cigarettes or other nicotine-containing products faster than originally intended. Although over 80% of individuals who smoke express a desire to stop smoking and 35% try to stop each year, less than 5% are successful in unaided attempts to quit. Spending a great deal of time in using the substance is best exemplified by chain-smoking. Because nicotine sources are readily and legally available, spending a great deal of time attempting to procure nicotine would be rare. Giving up important social, occupational, or recreational activities can occur when an individual forgoes an activity because it occurs in smoking-restricted areas. Continued use despite knowledge of medical problems related to smoking is a particularly important health problem (e.g., an individual who continues to smoke despite having a tobacco-induced general medical condition such as bronchitis or chronic obstructive lung disease).

Specifiers

The following specifiers may be applied to a diagnosis of Nicotine Dependence:

With Physiological Dependence
Without Physiological Dependence
Early Full Remission
Early Partial Remission
Sustained Full Remission
Sustained Partial Remission
On Agonist Therapy

Nicotine-Induced Disorder

292.0   Nicotine Withdrawal

The essential feature of Nicotine Withdrawal is the presence of a characteristic withdrawal syndrome that develops after the abrupt cessation of, or reduction in, the use of nicotine-containing products following a prolonged period (at least several weeks) of daily use (Criteria A and B). The withdrawal syndrome includes four or more of the following: dysphoric or depressed mood; insomnia; irritability, frustration, or anger; anxiety; diffi-
(Continued)

culty concentrating; restlessness or impatience; decreased heart rate; and increased appetite or weight gain. The withdrawal symptoms cause clinically significant distress or impairment in social, occupational, or other important areas of functioning (Criterion C). The symptoms must not be due to a general medical condition and are not better accounted for by another mental disorder (Criterion D).

These symptoms are in large part due to nicotine deprivation and are typically more intense among individuals who smoke cigarettes than among individuals who use other nicotine-containing products. The more rapid onset of nicotine effects with cigarette smoking leads to a more intensive habit pattern that is more difficult to give up because of the frequency and rapidity of reinforcement and the greater physical dependence on nicotine. In individuals who smoke cigarettes, heart rate decreases by 5 to 12 beats per minute in the first few days after stopping smoking, and weight increases an average of 2–3 kg over the first year after stopping smoking. Mild symptoms of withdrawal may occur after switching to low-tar/nicotine cigarettes and after stopping the use of smokeless (chewing) tobacco, nicotine gum, or nicotine patches.

Diagnostic criteria for 292.0 Nicotine Withdrawal

A. Daily use of nicotine for at least several weeks.

B. Abrupt cessation of nicotine use, or reduction in the amount of nicotine used, followed within 24 hours by four (or more) of the following signs:

  (1) dysphoric or depressed mood
  (2) insomnia
  (3) irritability, frustration, or anger
  (4) anxiety
  (5) difficulty concentrating
  (6) restlessness
  (7) decreased heart rate
  (8) increased appetite or weight gain

C. The symptoms in Criterion B cause clinically significant distress or impairment in social, occupational, or other important areas of functioning.

D. The symptoms are not due to a general medical condition and are not better accounted for by another mental disorder.

Additional Information on Nicotine-Related Disorders

Associated Features and Disorders

Associated descriptive features and mental disorders. Craving is an important element in Nicotine Withdrawal and may account for the difficulty that individuals have in giving up nicotine-containing products. Other symptoms associated with Nicotine Withdrawal include a desire for sweets and impaired performance on tasks requiring vigilance. Several features associated with Nicotine Dependence appear to predict a greater level of difficulty in stopping nicotine use: smoking soon after waking, smoking when ill, difficulty refraining from smoking, reporting the first cigarette of the day to be the one most difficult to give up, and smoking more in the morning than in the afternoon. The number of cigarettes smoked per day, the nicotine yield of the cigarette, and the number of pack-years also are related to the likelihood of an individual stopping smoking. Nicotine Dependence is more common among individuals with other mental disorders. Depending on the population studied, from 55% to 90% of individuals with other mental disorders smoke, compared to 30% in the general population. Mood, Anxiety, and other Substance-Related Disorders may be more common in individuals who smoke than in those who are ex-smokers and those who have never smoked.

Associated laboratory findings. Withdrawal symptoms are associated with a slowing on EEG, decreases in catecholamine and cortisol levels, rapid eye movement (REM) changes, impairment on neuropsychological testing, and decreased metabolic rate. Smoking increases the metabolism of many medications prescribed for the treatment of mental disorders and of other substances. Thus, cessation of smoking can increase the blood levels of these medications and other substances, sometimes to a clinically significant degree. This effect does not appear to be due to nicotine but rather to other compounds in tobacco. Nicotine and its metabolite cotinine can be measured in blood, saliva, or urine. Persons who smoke also often have diminished pulmonary function tests and increased mean corpuscular volume (MCV).

Associated physical examination findings and general medical conditions. Nicotine Withdrawal may be associated with a dry or productive cough, de-
(Continued)

creased heart rate, increased appetite or weight gain, and a dampened orthostatic response. The most common signs of Nicotine Dependence are tobacco odor, cough, evidence of chronic obstructive pulmonary disease, and excessive skin wrinkling. Tobacco stains on the fingers can occur but are rare. Tobacco use can markedly increase the risk of lung, oral, and other cancers; cardiovascular and cerebrovascular conditions; chronic obstructive and other lung diseases; ulcers; maternal and fetal complications; and other conditions. Although most of these problems appear to be caused by the carcinogens and carbon monoxide in tobacco smoke rather than by nicotine itself, nicotine may increase the risk for cardiovascular events. Those who have never smoked but are chronically exposed to tobacco smoke appear to be at increased risk for conditions such as lung cancer and heart disease.

Specific Culture, Age, and Gender Features

The prevalence of smoking is decreasing in most industrialized nations, but is increasing in the developing areas. In the United States, the prevalence of smoking is slightly higher in males than in females; however, the prevalence of smoking is decreasing more rapidly in males than in females. In other countries, smoking is often much more prevalent among males.

Prevalence

In the United States, approximately 45% of the general population have never smoked. The remainder fall into one or more of the following categories: 25% are ex-smokers, 30% currently smoke cigarettes, 4% use pipes or cigars, and 3% use smokeless tobacco. In the United States, the prevalence of smoking has been decreasing approximately 0.7%–1.0% per year. The lifetime prevalence of Nicotine Dependence in the general population is estimated to be 20%. In the United States, between 50% and 80% of individuals who currently smoke have Nicotine Dependence. Lifetime prevalence of Nicotine Withdrawal among persons who smoke appears to be about 50%. Prospectively, it is estimated that about 50% of those who quit smoking on their own and about 75% of those in treatment programs experience Nicotine Withdrawal when they stop smoking.

Course

Smoking usually begins in the early teens. How quickly dependence develops is unclear. Among those who continue to smoke through age 20 years, 95% become regular, daily smokers. Of those who successfully quit, less than 25% quit on their first attempt. Most individuals who smoke have 3–4 failures before they stop smoking for good. In the United States, about 45% of those who have ever smoked eventually stop smoking. Withdrawal symptoms can begin within a few hours of cessation, typically peak in 1–4 days, and last for 3–4 weeks. Depressive symptoms postcessation may be associated with a relapse to smoking. Whether other Nicotine Withdrawal symptoms play a major role in relapse to smoking is debatable. Increased hunger and weight gain often persist for at least 6 months. Six months postcessation, 50% of individuals who have quit smoking report having had a desire for a cigarette in the last 24 hours.

Familial Pattern

The risk for smoking increases threefold if a first-degree biological relative smokes. Twin and adoption studies indicate that genetic factors contribute to the onset and continuation of smoking, with the degree of heritability equivalent to that observed with Alcohol Dependence.

Differential Diagnosis

The symptoms of Nicotine Withdrawal overlap with those of other substance withdrawal syndromes; Caffeine Intoxication; Anxiety, Mood, and Sleep Disorders; and medication-induced akathisia. Admission to smoke-free inpatient units can induce withdrawal symptoms that might mimic, intensify, or disguise other diagnoses. Reduction of symptoms associated with the resumption of smoking or nicotine-replacement therapy confirms the diagnosis.

Because regular nicotine use does not appear to impair mental functioning, Nicotine Dependence is not readily confused with other Substance-Related Disorders and mental disorders.

292.9   Nicotine-Related Disorder Not Otherwise Specified

The Nicotine-Related Disorder Not Otherwise Specified category is for disorders associated with the use of nicotine that are not classifiable as Nicotine Dependence or Nicotine Withdrawal.

Source: Adapted, with permission, from *Diagnostic and Statistical Manual of Mental Disorders*, Fourth Edition. Copyright 1994 by the American Psychiatric Association.

are studies indicating that certain psychotropic drugs can have a beneficial effect on smoking behavior (see Chapter 6). The real danger is in not recognizing that those who continue to smoke in the face of clear-cut evidence of its dangers are not recognized as needing psychiatric treatment.

Does this mean that anyone who smokes is mentally ill? While many may say "yes," the answer is that smokers are more like those with other addictions than a separate population. They have, in fact, suffered the same loss of control in their dopaminergic systems that is common to illicit drug users. In addition, their potential to suffer from major depression or other anxiety disorders makes them a more vulnerable population suffering from comorbidity and even less likely to succeed in a treatment program that does not recognize their level of "double trouble."[18]

The fact that nicotine does provide some perceived benefit from increased alertness and performance enhancement makes its psychological hold even more virulent. This area requires more study.[15]

References

1. Fischer PM, Schwartz MP, Richard JW et al. Brand logo recognition by children aged 3 to 6 years. *JAMA*. 1991;266(22):3145–3148.
2. Robinson JH, Pritchard WS. The role of nicotine in tobacco use. *Psychopharmacology*. 1992;108:397–407.
3. Frith CD. Smoking behaviour and its relation to the smoker's immediate experience. *Br J Soc Clin Psychol*. 1971;10:73–78.
4. Warburton DM. Heroin, Cocaine, and now nicotine. In Warburton D (ed.) *Addiction Controversies*. London: Harwood, 1990, pp 21–35.
5. West R. Nicotine addiction: A re-analysis of the arguments. commentary. *Psychopharmacology*. 1992;108:408–410.
6. U.S. Department of Health and Human Services. *Preventing Tobacco Use among Young People: A Report of the Surgeon General*. Atlanta, Ga: U.S. Department of Health and Human Services, Public Health Service, Centers for Disease Control and Prevention, National Center for

Chronic Disease Prevention and Health Promotion, Office on Smoking and Health, 1994.

7. Henningfield JE, Cohen C, Slade JD. Is nicotine more addictive than cocaine? *Brit J Addiction*. 1991;86(5):565–569.

8. Evans NJ, Gilpin E, Pierce JP et al. Occasional smoking among adults: Evidence from the California Tobacco Survey. *Tobacco Control*. 1992; 1(3):169–175.

9. Henningfield JE. Occasional drug use: Comparing nicotine with other addictive drugs. *Tobacco Control*. 1992;1(3):161–162.

10. Kozlowski LT, Henningfield JE, Keenan RM et al. Patterns of alcohol, cigarette, and caffeine and other drug use in two drug abusing populations. *J Substance Abuse Treat*. 1993;10(2):171–179.

11. Centers for Disease Control and Prevention. Smoking cessation during previous year among adults—United States, 1990 and 1991. *Morbidity and Mortality Weekly Report 1993a;*42(26):504–507.

12. US Department of Health and Human Services. *The health consequences of smoking: Nicotine addiction. A report of the Surgeon General, 1988.* US Department of Health and Human Services, Public Health Service, Centers for Disease Control, Center for Health Promotion and Education, Office on Smoking and Health, DHHS Publication No. (CDC) 88-8406, 1988.

13. Henningfield JE, Clayton R, Pollin N. Involvement of tobacco in alcoholism and illicit drug use. *British Journal of Addiction*. 1990; 85(2):279–292.

14. Where there's smoke . . . Nicotine and psychiatric disorders. Editorial. *Biol Psychiatry*. 1991;30:107–108.

15. Jarvik ME, Schneider NG. Nicotine. In Lowinson JH, Ruiz P, Millman RB, and Langrod J, eds., *Substance Abuse: Comprehensive Textbook*. Baltimore: Williams & Wilkins, 1992.

16. News from the Council on Research. *Psychiatr Res Rep*, January 1994.

17. Kennedy JA, Crowley TJ, Cottler LB, et al. Substance use diagnoses in smokers with lung disease. *Am J Addictions*. 1993;2(2):126–129.

18. Glassman AH. Cigarette smoking: Implications for psychiatric illness. *Am J Psychiatr*. 1993;150(4):546–553.

19. Mansnerus L. Smoking: Is it a habit or is it genetic? *New York Times*, October 4, 1992.

20. Breslau N, Kilbey MM, Andreski P. Nicotine withdrawal symptoms

and psychiatric disorders: Findings from an epidemiologic study of young adults. *Am J Psychiatr*. 1992;149(4):464–469.

21. Hughes JR, Hatsukami DK, Mitchell JE et al. Prevalence of smoking among psychiatric outpatients. *Am J Psychiatr*. 1986;143:993–997.

22. Goff DC, Henderson DC, Amico E. Cigarette smoking in schizophrenia: Relationship to psychopathology and medication side effects. *Am J Psychiatr*. 1992;149:1189–1194

23. Perkins KA, Epstein LH, Grobe J et al. Tobacco abstinence, smoking cues, and the reinforcing value of smoking. *Pharmacol Biochem Behav*. 1994;47:107–112.

24. West R, Lennox A. Function of cigarette smoking in relation to examinations. *Psychopharmacology*. 1992;108:456–459.

25. Landers DM. Crews DJ, Boutcher SH et al. The effects of smokeless tobacco on performance and psychophysiological response. *Medicine and Science in Sports and Exercise*. 1992;895–903.

26. Newhouse PA, Potter A, Corwin J, Lenox R. Acute nicotinic blockade produces cognitive impairment in normal humans. *Psychopharmacology*. 1992;108:480–484.

27. Pritchard WS, Robinson JH, Guy TD. Enhancement of continuous performance task reaction time by smoking in non-deprived smokers. *Psychopharmacology*. 1992;108:437–442.

28. Warburton DM, Rusted JM, Fowler J. A comparison of the attentional and consolidation hypotheses for the facilitation of memory by nicotine. *Psychopharmacology*. 1992;108:443–447.

29. Nicotine May Help Rats Remember to Pay Attention. Health: (need complete reference)

30. Gritz ER, Carr CR, Marcus AC. The tobacco withdrawal syndrome in unaided quitters. *Br J Addiction*. 1991;86(1):57–69.

31. West R, Schneider N. Craving for cigarettes. *Br J Addiction*. 1987; 82:407–415.

32. Rose JE, Levin ED. Inter-relationships between conditioned and primary reinforcement in the maintenance of cigarette smoking. *Br J Addiction*. 1991;86:605–609.

33. Herskovic JE, Rose JE, Jarvik ME. Cigarette desirability and nicotine preference in smokers. *Pharmacol Biochem Behav*. 1986;24:171–175.

34. Rose JE. The role of upper airway stimulation in smoking. In Pomerlaeau OF, Pomerleau CS, eds. *Nicotine replacement: A critical evaluation*. New York: Liss, 1988.

35. Hasenfratz M, Baldinger B et al. Nicotine or tar titration in cigarette smoking behavior. *Psychopharmacology*. 1993;112:253–258.
36. Perkins KA, Grobe JE, Epstein LH et al. Chronic and acute tolerance to subjective effects of nicotine. *Pharmacol Biochem Behav*. 1993;45:1–7.
37. Fagerstron KO, Schneider NG. Measuring nicotine dependence: A review of the Fagerstrom Tolerance Questionnaire. *J Behav Med*. 1989;12(2):159–182.
38. Larson PS, Haas HB Silvette H. Tobacco experimental and clinical studies. Baltimore: Williams & Wilkins, 1961.
39. Larson PS, Haas HB, Silvette H. Tobacco, experimental and clinical studies, Supplement I. Baltimore: Williams & Wilkins, 1968.
40. Larson PS, Haas HB, Silvette H. Tobacco, experimental and clinical studies, Supplement II. Baltimore: Williams & Wilkins, 1971.
41. Larson PS, Haas HB, Silvette H. Tobacco: Experimental and clinical studies, Supplement III. Baltimore: Williams & Wilkins, 1975.
42. Snyder PR, Henningfield JE. Effects of nicotine administration following 12 h of tobacco deprivation: Assessment on computerized performance tasks. *Psychopharmacology*. 1989;97:17–22.
43. Herning RI, Pickworth WB. Nicotine gum improved stimulus processing during tobacco withdrawal. *Psychophysiology*. 1985;22:594.
44. Schneider NG, Jarvik ME, Forsythe AB. Nicotine vs. placebo gum in the alleviation of withdrawal during smoking cessation. *Addict Behav*. 1984;9:149–156.

Additional Sources

Epstein LH, Bulik CM, Perkins KA et al. Behavioral economic analysis of smoking: Money and food as alternatives. *Pharmacol Biochem Behav*. 1991;38:715–721.

Dalack GW, Glassman AH, Rivelli S et al. Mood, major depression and fluoxetine response in cigarette smokers. Presented at New Research Poster Session at 145th Annual Meeting of the American Psychiatric Association, May 2–7, 1992.

DSM-III-R. *Diagnostic and Statistical Manual of Mental Disorders*, 3rd ed. rev. Washington, DC: American Psychiatric Association, 1987.

Mensa MA, Grossman N, Van Horn M et al. Smoking and movement disorders in psychiatric patients. 1991;300:109–115.

6

Treatment and the Role
of the Physician

Every year almost three-quarters of the nation's 46 million smokers vow to stop. But very few do. In fact, those that can quit easily already have quit. And for those who keep trying, there is no shortage of programs available. There are a myriad of options, from proprietary ones like Smokenders to programs sponsored by nonprofit organizations and local groups such as the American Cancer Society and the YMCA.

The Surgeon General has stated that a simple, easy way to reduce smoking would be to make the economic price as painful as the health care cost. The SG estimates that every 10% increase in the cost of cigarettes reduces demand by 4%. However, even if there was a tax increase raising the price of cigarettes to $5 per pack, an estimated 15 billion packs would still be sold each year![1]

But a radical tax increase on cigarettes is probably not going to occur in the near future, and millions of people will continue to light up. As the research evidence continues to mount against tobacco, it becomes more and more apparent that physicians should be taking the lead in their practices and their communities to get people to stop or never to start smoking. After all, smoking is our number one public health problem.

Beyond the role of the physician in promoting "wellness," there are many sound clinical reasons for practitioners in all specialties to be focused on smoking cessation.

One obvious reason is that a physician is probably the most influential person to frequently interact with high-risk patients who smoke, providing multiple opportunities for education. Another clear reason is that, as previous chapters clearly demonstrate, the diagnosis of both primary and secondary conditions is often influenced by nicotine addiction or the by-products of tobacco smoke. And of course, whether a patient smokes impacts on the prognosis and treatment regimens for almost any disorder.[2]

Can a physician really make a difference? The answer is yes.

There is some evidence that we face a much more difficult task today than in the past, since most of the smokers who have already quit did so relatively easily on their own. The patients whom physicians must intervene with today are heavier users with higher levels of addiction or comorbid conditions that can complicate attempts at abstinence. Many experts also believe that nicotine addiction is the sole reason why people do not or cannot stop smoking, so the approach to these patients must be both medical and behavioral. There are, however, some things in favor of any attempt to reduced smoking levels by any practitioner:

According to a 1993 Gallup poll, 68% of respondents were at least somewhat interested in quitting; of those, 30% were very interested. Among respondents who wanted to quit, 76% cited concern about health risks as a major reason. So, in general, most patients will be premotivated. Physicians, even if they are in a small or limited practice, can be effective simply by screening all patients for tobacco use. They can provide one-to-one information on health risks to a "captive audience," and they are in a position to do effective follow-up. Physicians can determine those patients who need psychiatric or other mental health counseling and help structure a medical-pharmacological intervention.[1]

But there is, at the very least, a "perception gap" among patients as to the role of their own physician and the knowledge transmitted about the health problems caused by cigarettes. Although 61% of smokers said their physicians had advised them to quit, 49% said their doctors did not offer a stop-smoking program or did not discuss, in detail, the detrimental effects of smoking. For example, 25% of the Gallup smokers did not relate tobacco use to heart disease, 35% did not realize that smoking could lead to strokes, and 16% did not link smoking and lung cancer.[3]

Does the level of smoking addiction make a difference in the potential for success? The experts aren't sure.

"I think the jury is still out on that, although it may make some intuitive sense," says Thomas P. Houston, M.D., director of the American Medical Association's department of preventive medicine and public health.[3]

John P. Pierce, Ph.D., director of cancer prevention at the University of California at San Diego, and former chief of epidemiology of the Office of Smoking and Health for the CDC, says, "I don't believe there is any conclusive evidence that people are resisting the public health pressure not to smoke because of increased addiction."[3]

In an 18-month study of 4400 current and former smokers that he conducted in California, Pierce found that stopping "cold turkey" may not work any better than other cessation techniques and programs. Cessation success rates for people who had stopped smoking for seven or more days during the past year or had successfully quit smoking for at least a year (positive histories), in spite of relapses, were similar to those achieved by people with "low addiction levels" who smoked under 15 cigarettes a day. People with positive histories and low addiction levels had a success rate of 30%, while people with heavier addictions and no positive histories had much lower success rates.

"This is significant," says Pierce, "because now you can tell patients that they can make progress toward quitting, even if they try and fail. If they attempt to quit, try to get them to stop for at least a week. If they start smoking again, try to get them to cut back to less than 15 a day. If you can, their chances of success will be better."[3]

The Challenge to the Medical Profession

Physicians have to take a role in smoking cessation that is clear and unambiguous. If they don't clearly, directly discourage smoking, then the message is clouded. To some extent, physicians may not fully understand how to reduce tobacco and other substance abuse among difficult patient groups. When the nicotine patch was approved, it was quickly accepted as a panacea, and over seven million prescriptions were filled in one year (1992). But the patch was designed to be used in a total cessation program that utilizes behavioral modification and other techniques to overcome nicotine addiction, not by itself. As a result success rates were disappointing, and doubts about the "patch effect" arose for the wrong reasons.

In the end, the toughest job for the physician may be just getting and keeping the attention of their patients.

Says Houston, "Smokers tend to have selective hearing. They hear what they want to hear. . . . but also, maybe not enough of us (physicians) are giving a clear, unequivocal message to quit. . . . The whole crux of the AMA's clinical guidelines is to ask every patient his or her smoking status, advise every patient to quit, be ready to provide assistance to those who want to quit, arrange to follow up with those who do want to leave Tobacco Road and, in the case of adolescents, learn to anticipate the threat of tobacco."[3]

Pierce agrees: "For physicians, just giving advice is useless."[3]

Data indicate that almost 75% of all smokers see a physician each year, giving practitioners a focused period of time to begin intervention. If only a small percentage of these interventions worked—perhaps as small as 10%—then several million people each year might be on their way to stopping. Physician–patient interaction can be successful. Few people doubt the credibility of their doctor, and his or her intervention can make the difference.

Lack of training, time, a back-up staff, and a program that works can be roadblocks for practitioner-based cessation programs. However, there are many resources, both in the community and among professional colleagues, that can be used for a successful approach. Studies have demonstrated that stop-smoking programs are not single events; they must become a routine aspect of daily practice to be successful.[4]

Getting a Program Off the Ground

Any smoking-cessation program is a mixed bag of pharmacological, behavioral, and other treatment procedures. The following outlines some broad issues to consider in a practice-based smoking cessation and treatment program.

To a great extent, the patient's concomitant health and psychiatric condition determines the extent and type of treatment program. There are, however, some commonalities that all physicians will encounter when assisting smoking cessation.

There are also "model" programs provided by the National Cancer Institute and other nonprofit organizations that practitioners can obtain free of charge and utilize as the basis of their own office- or community-based program. These are described fully in Chapter 7.

Prior to establishing a smoking cessation program, it is vital to understand that almost all smokers have some general concerns that will almost always be present. Among the most common are:

"I can't quit because I'll get fat!"
Most people who stop smoking gain weight—usually 5–10 pounds. As a result, there is a common perception that when you stop smoking, you have to instantly begin dieting. This means that the body—not to mention the mind—will have to perform double duty. Patients should view ending smoking as the beginning of a

healthful lifestyle. Instead of dieting, exercise, better eating, and the possible use of the patch or nicotine gum for a period of time will mitigate withdrawal symptoms. The fact is that a person would have to gain 100 pounds to put himself or herself at a risk as bad as that of smoking.

"Even if I quit, everyone else in the family is still smoking. It's hard to stop when everyone else hasn't."

Overcoming any addiction requires a strong family support system. Nicotine addiction is no different. Quitting becomes even more difficult when a spouse smokes, not to mention various extended family members. Even nonsmokers may be codependents, thinking the smoker should smoke. There are things that can be done, for example, setting a smoke free zone in the house or getting family members to pledge not to smoke in the presence of the former smoker. However, in the end, the best approach is to work with the entire family to reduce smoking levels.[2]

"Smoking just makes me feel better. I need to smoke at certain times, and giving it up would be worse than what happens to me when I'm old."

Practitioners and friends of smokers hear this rationale more than any other. Like any addict in denial, smoking is a way of life and part of the addict's lifestyle. The reinforcing effects of nicotine, along with the "conditioned responses" to places and situations where smoking occurs, are a "very powerful deterrent to cessation. In addition, people often smoke in social situations where there are other smokers or where smoking is not discouraged: bars, dances, or other venues with positive connotations. As if this weren't enough, the smoker is bombarded by conflicting messages about smoking from industry advocates and health care specialists. The "noise level" surrounding smoking can be deafening. So, the solution for many is to reach for a relatively low cost, always available solution: a pack of cigarettes.

Practitioners can overcome some of these attitudes by understanding that pharmacological interventions don't overcome the behavioral aspects of craving and compulsive use. So, providing the "long-term view" while treating the short-term effects is an important role for any practitioner involved in intervention. Physicians should encourage their patients to try to be patient, telling them that those who do eventually stop smoking report that they are happier and calmer as nonsmokers.[5]

"I want to stop, but every time I try, I just can't seem to stick with it."

Often physicians see patients who want to stop but just can't seem to remain motivated. Dr. Teressa Moyers, Ph.D., of the University of New Mexico in Albuquerque (ASAM, NYC, 1994) suggests various techniques, including motivational interviewing, which attempts to increase the person's motivation to change.

Many smokers quit on their own, and studying them has led to Prochask and DiClemente's notions of how people stop smoking and change on their own and how we can help those who need our help to stop.

Motivational interviewing doesn't work for everyone, but it can help people who are in denial or minimize their problems. Prochaska and DiClemente say that they enter the wheel of change from precontemplation ("I really don't think that my smoking is causing my problem") to contemplation ("I have to do something about my smoking; although I really do not think it is hurting me, I think that I should") to preparation or determination ("I intend to change") to action ("I have stopped smoking on my own, but I think that I may need additional help") to maintenance ("I have stopped smoking for weeks, but I am just hanging on and could slip at any time") to relapse ("I failed, and I do not know whether I am ready to try again").

Denial or ambivalence is normal. The clinician sees that this person needs to change and change now, but the patient is still in the contemplation stage. People who are thinking that they should stop smoking ("My child is allergic, and I'm thinking that I should stop") should have motivational counseling to help them achieve a higher motivational level to change their smoking behavior. Specific coping strategies, prescriptions, or advice work best.

Clinical Opportunities to Talk about Smoking with Patients

Symptoms

Cough
Sputum production
Shortness of breath

Tests

Electrocardiography
Pulmonary function tests
Total leukocyte counts
Blood pressure measurements
Hematocrit
Auscultation of heart and lungs = blood lipid studies
Blood coagulation studies
Serum alpha$_1$ antiprotease determinations
Pregnancy tests
Carboxyhemoglobin determinations

Diagnosis of Disease and Risk Factors

Coronary heart disease
Peripheral vascular disease
Angina pectoris
Hypertension
Emphysema
Chronic bronchitis
Pneumonia
Asthma
Acute bronchitis
Recurrent respiratory infection
Diabetes mellitus
Hypercholesterolemia
Peptic ulcer
Allergy

Drug Prescriptions

Drug–tobacco-smoke interactions
Pharmacological aids to smoking cessation

Source: *Clinical Opportunities for Smoking Intervention: A Guide for the Busy Physician.* U.S. Department of Health and Human Services, Public Health Service, National Institutes of Health, 1986.

Provoke the following in each patient:

Precontemplation. "These are your test results. These are the norms. You need to think about your health."

Contemplation. "What do you gain by smoking? What are your risks?" You can even say, "Perhaps you really do not have a problem. Perhaps you should just stay the same." The ambivalent person normally then takes the opposite argument for change. Individuals who can verbalize positive benefits from change are most likely to succeed. Ask, "What do you want to accomplish by stopping?" A direct confrontation is often the worst approach for the ambivalent person.

Action. Patients have agreed to change. Present options for treatment and group treatment, and remove barriers to treatment.

Relapse. Demystify and explain relapse versus slips: "Most people slip and still succeed in stopping." Identify the specific things that led to the relapse and what can be done to prevent them in the future.

Maintenance. "These are the things that you can do with all of your spare time, money, and energy."
In addition, rather than just confrontation and advice, empathy is necessary, but you still need other skills and techniques. The more people accept themselves as they are, the more is their ability to move on and change. Ambivalence and resistance are normal but can be overcome with counseling.

Empathy is a good place to start with the person in the contemplation phase of smoking cessation. Help people understand and become aware of the consequences so that they have a discrepancy between what they want for themselves in the next month, year, and five years and how is that different from where they are going. Use the costs and benefits of smoking. Make a list and balance.

In a motivational interview, tell people that they are not powerless to change, that they are the most important factor in change, that they are in control of whether they succeed or fail, and that you can only "lead a horse to water."

Confrontation has a role, but people can always do what they want to do, since we cannot be with them 24 hours a day for a year or for life. You can even temporarily tolerate people that you know are lying to you to help them move out of the contemplation phase. Rather than accumulating facts, you need to see the smoking from their point of view, too. If a person says, "I am ready to change," he or she needs diagnosis, advice, information, and treatment. However, if the person is really ambivalent, motivational interviewing should come first.

Diagnosis: The First Step

Any good treatment program—especially one that has to overcome resistance—must begin with a strong diagnostic approach, and here the smoker can help you out. Unlike addicts who abuse illicit drugs or alcohol, smokers are almost always forthcoming about their smoking habits. While they may deny the dangers, few deny use.[6]

Some of the steps are obvious and follow any approach to treatment:

- Take a solid history documenting tobacco use patterns, attempts to stop, and related issues (family support, etc.) that may contribute to treatment resistance. A heavy user is going to have a more difficult time stopping, so these questions, although obvious, may be vital in choosing a course of intervention.
- Examine concomitant health problems that affect the potential for pharmacological intervention, as well as comorbid situations such as alcohol or drug dependency.
- Ask more targeted questions about smoking patterns such as the type of cigarette (light, menthol, filtered, etc.).
- Assess patient's baseline level of medical or scientific knowledge, which will give the practitioner an understand-

---

The Vital Office Visit

Michael Fiore, an internist and tobacco treatment specialist, recently suggested that doctors modify their office visit procedures to include smoking assessment. For example, a required part of every office visit is to expand the vital signs assessment by a nurse to include smoking status. Today only 50% of smokers say that they have been asked about their smoking by their doctor or his/her staff. Just print the information on the vital signs part of the medical record. While the clinician's intervention may cause a success rate of only 5%, what other chronic disease can be cured every year by a simple intervention?

The doctor needs to say something to the effect of "a single puff in the first two weeks will cause relapse." By using the annual doctor visit, 2 million people a year can successfully stop, even with a 5% annual success rate. Adding excise taxes, environmental protection to ban indoor smoking, and social stigma makes this time a propitious one, when many patients are in a state where there is a window of opportunity to quit.

Source: Michael Fiore, MD, a tobacco specialist and internist at the University of Wisconsin. 25th Conference of the American Society of Addiction Medicine, April 13–17, 1994, New York, New York.

---

ing of the patient's basic attitudes toward tobacco. For example, the approach to a patient who says, "I know it's not good, but I can't stop" will be different from the program for the patient who says, "I never believe what I read about cigarettes. If they were really bad, they wouldn't be legal."[5]

Along with a basic history, there is a range of diagnostic tests and procedures that can be used.

Fagerstrom Test

The Fagerstrom Tolerance Questionnaire[7] is a simple pen-and-paper, self-assessment test that measures nicotine addiction. It's frequently used in both research and clinical environments. The Fagerstrom test is most useful in predicting smoking cessation outcomes in individual patients. It is also helpful in choosing patients who will respond to nicotine replacement therapy, the type of therapy, and the level of medication needed. Another self-report test is Horn's Reason for Smoking Test, which measures individual differences in smoking patterns.[6]

Patient Profile

Fagerstrom Tolerance Questionnaire (FTQ)*

Questions	Answers	Points
1. How soon after you wake up do you smoke your first cigarette?	Within 30 minutes After 30 minutes	1 0
2. Do you find it difficult to refrain from smoking in places where it is forbidden?	Yes No	1 0
3. Which cigarette would hate most to give up?	The first one in the morning Any other	1 0
4. How many cigarettes/day do you smoke?	15 or less 16–25 25 or more	0 2
5. Do you smoke more frequently during the first hours after awakening than during the rest of the day?	Yes No	1 0
6. Do you smoke if you are so ill that you are in bed most of the day?	Yes No	1 0
7. What is the nicotine level of your usual brand of cigarette?	0.9 mg or less 1.0–1.2 mg 1.3 mg or more	0 1 2
8. Do you inhale?	Never Sometimes Always	0 1 2

*The FTQ has a scoring range of 0–11 points, with a score of 0 assumed indicative of minimum nicotine dependence and a score of 11 indicative of maximum nicotine dependence. The mean score is usually within the range of 5–7 points, with a standard deviation of about 2. For an unselected group of smokers, the mean score is about 5 or 6 (Opinion Research Corp., 1988); for smokers asking for treatment, the mean is usually between 6 and 7 (Fagerstrom and Schneider, 1989).

Cotinine Test

One potential future method of assessing nicotine dependence, which may be complicated, is measuring biological markers, particularly *cotinine*, which is a specific and important metabolite associated with nicotine. It could provide a numerical reading that correlates to smoking risk that can be presented to the patient, just the way blood sugar or cholesterol readings are used.[7]

Assessing the Practitioner's Role: Step Two

There is, of course, a need to be realistic when devising a cessation program. While physicians can provide effective treatment, they can't be all things to all patients. It is essential to assess the limits of your influence with each patient individually, so that you remain effective.

There are some very specific functions the clinician should be providing:

- Clearly, once nicotine dependency treatment begins, the physician should monitor the patient for withdrawal distress so that possible pharmacological intervention can be provided. If the patient is abstinent and complaining of withdrawal symptoms, the physician might prescribe one of the transdermal nicotine patches or the clonidine patch.
- The physician can encourage the patient to attend Nicotine Anonymous, use the telephone rather than a cigarette, and join highly structured relapse prevention groups.
- The physician can mobilize the family to support and improve compliance and reduce relapse. By closely monitoring success of outpatient treatment, the physician can identify persistent nonresponders and refer them for residential nicotine dependence treatment.[1]

There are also some general aspects of intervention that the physician can present, molding, picking and choosing those that fit his or her practice situation and style best.

The National Institutes for Health has suggested the following five "clinical opportunities for smoking intervention" in its *Guide for the Busy Physician.*[2]

1. Act as a role model. Adopt a no-smoking policy for your office staff. Studies show that a high proportion of nurses continue to smoke. Display "No Smoking" signs or posters in your waiting room. Remove ashtrays from the waiting area. Include pamphlets about the health effects of smoking and smoking cessation among your waiting room reading materials.

2. Provide information on risks. Patients need specific information about how their smoking affects their health and how their health might be improved if they stop smoking. Smoking can also have profound effects on diagnostic test results and on therapeutic drug absorption, metabolism, and action. In fact, when you are administering a test or conducting a routine procedure, you have an opportunity to educate your patient about the effects of smoking.

3. Encourage abstinence by direct advice and suggestions. When you talk with your patients, you should be brief, direct, unambiguous, and informative. What you tell patients about smoking should not be used as a "scare tactic." The kind of smoking behavior your patient has and his or her feelings about quitting should influence the advice you give and the action steps you suggest. The Fagerstrom Tolerance Questionnaire may help you identify nicotine dependent smokers.

The age of the patient may help shape your approach to smoking intervention. An adolescent is not likely to be influenced by a discussion of the long-term risks of smoking. But he or she may be motivated to quit if persuaded that smoking will have an effect on sports performance or social desirability.

One behavioral step that is often recommended to help smokers quit is to set a quit smoking date. Even smokers with an excellent quitting prognosis may be unwilling to make such a commitment. If the patient does not want to set a date, suggest that he or she take some other positive action within a specified time frame: contact a smoking-cessation program or think over your message and talk to you about it again.

Approximately 60% of adult smokers have made at least one serious attempt to give up cigarettes but have relapsed. Most smokers succeed only after making several attempts to quit. Smokers who have tried and failed to quit need to know this. There are a variety of reasons why people relapse, but usually you can anticipate and cope with most of them. It is important, for example, to tell patients that they may experience physical withdrawal symptoms when they first stop smoking. A positive "can-do" attitude seems to correlate with success in stopping smoking.

4. Refer patients to a smoking-cessation program. Most communities have effective behavioral programs to help smokers give up the habit. Self-help materials are also available.

5. Follow-up. Patients who complete community programs or try to stop smoking on their own can benefit from physician advice that reinforces their program's behavior change messages. Your continual support and encouragement are crucial. For efficient follow-up:

- Flag the charts of smokers and former smokers to remind yourself to ask about smoking at each visit.
- Continue to give individual health messages to patients who are still smoking.
- Try again to get each patient who smokes to set a quit date, accept referral to a group program, or use self-help materials.
- Schedule support visits to reinforce a patient's decision to quit, deal with withdrawal, and discuss other relevant concerns. Such visits are especially important during the first four to eight weeks of a quitting program.
- Follow up by calling the patient or by setting a time for the patient to call you. When a patient feels that you care about his or her progress, it improves the chances that he or she will quit successfully.

Physicians may want to involve their staff in the office-based program, for example, by putting a nurse or other staff person in charge of additional information and support for the smoker. There is evidence that counseling from both a physician and a nurse who is well informed and possesses good "people" skills can increase success rates.[8]

Devising the Program: Step Three

Quitting smoking for millions of people has been easy. They just stopped on their own. But they are the lucky ones. Those who can't quit on their own and try every type of program from acupuncture to clinics to plastic replacement cigarettes relapse at a rate of 70%–80%.[9] One reason for the high relapse rate is the highly individual nature of smoking: There is no typical smoker, and there is no program that seems to have a lock on the right combination of behavioral and pharmacological elements.

Most recently, smoking-cessation programs have focused on reduction of nicotine dependence rather than "unlearning" to smoke. This combination of techniques has raised success rates in some cases to 50%.[10] Most experts agree that stand-alone smoking-cessation programs, overall, rarely achieve success rates higher than 10%–20%. However, combined approaches can raise these success rates often as high as 40%–50%.[11]

There are a number of program models to choose from, but regardless of their depth and scope, they will have to encompass some very specific options that spin out of the diagnostic process, coupled with the role that the practitioner chooses.

The physician needs to be sensitive to the individual who is on the fence, helping her or him to the logical conclusion that stopping is vital. Those who have already decided to quit must be provided with options that will help them get through the initial withdrawal phase and stay on course, despite inevitable relapses.

Begin with educating all patients. A variety of behavioral and pharmacological therapies are available. Make sure that your follow-up procedures are in place. Can you make follow-up appointments in advance? Do you have referrals to support groups and other counseling services such as Nicotine Anonymous or other 12-step programs?

Often, programs begin by setting "quit dates" and "cut-down date" goals.[5] Typically, most programs last only a few days to a few weeks and focus on stopping, not relapse prevention. This is a key area for the practitioner to focus on.[11]

Above all, whatever program is chosen, it must have a specific focus and be clearly outlined to the patients so they know what to expect.

Treatment Options: Step Four

Any program can combine one of the following four elements:

- Behavioral therapy
- Addiction treatment
- Pharmacological treatment
- Relapse prevention[12]

Behavioral Therapy

Behavioral therapy has worked for many people over the last several decades. It is, in effect, the core of any program. Teaching patients to cope with the urges and cues that put them in the endless circle of nicotine addiction also requires learning to handle stress without reaching for a cigarette and avoiding social situations that provoke habitual smoking until the first phase of abstinence is complete. Behavioral modification has been shown to be most effective in patients who are light smokers or who do not inhale deeply.[12]

In general, behavioral techniques do not succeed over the long haul,[9,13,14] with success rates at one year of from 15% to 30%. Most behavioral programs are too short (1 day to 6 weeks) and do not focus on long-term relapse prevention.[15] When a behavioral modification program is effective, it's because the smoker wants to quit. If smokers are willing to modify their lifestyle, change their smoking circle of friends, and have strong family support, behavioral modification can work. Learning to prevent relapses is the single most important part of these programs. Aversive conditioning techniques, including "rapid smoking, focus smoking, electric shock, and techniques such as covert sensitization of satiation," can work.[11]

One behavioral–adverse-conditioning program has successfully demonstrated the explicit risks of smoking through a carbon monoxide test on a patient's exhaled air. The high levels of toxic gas found in the bloodstream can be a dramatic example of the damage smokers are doing to themselves.[12]

Addiction Treatment

Addiction cannot be broken until denial is recognized and admitted by the addict. Nicotine is a particularly powerful drug. The practitioner who determines that multiple addictions are present (tobacco, alcohol, cocaine, etc.) must confront these issues with patients and turn them toward an evaluation, diagnosis, detoxification, intervention program and a 12-step or support group program.

Drug addiction of any kind will never cease until the drug addict changes her or his own view of the drug. There are a wide variety of inpatient and outpatient programs with pros and cons for each. Nicotine addiction does not require hospitalization; however, an outpatient program such as Smoker's Anonymous or Narcotics Anonymous will help smokers. Through each of these programs the smoker can get support and help in dealing with these key issues in smoking cessation:

- Identifying defense mechanisms
- Understanding nicotine craving
- Recognizing environmental cues

How People Change Addictive Behaviors

According to Prochaska et al., there are five stages of change:

1. *Precontemplation*: There is no intention to change behavior in the foreseeable future. Resistance to recognizing or modifying a problem is the hallmark of precontemplation.
2. *Contemplation*: There is an awareness that a problem exists and individuals are seriously thinking about overcoming it but have not yet made a commitment to take action. Serious consideration of problem resolution is the central element of contemplation.
3. *Preparation*: Combines intention and behavioral criteria. Individuals intend to take action in the next month and have unsuccessfully taken action in the past year (decision making).
4. *Action*: Individuals modify their behavior, experiences, or environment in order to overcome their problem. Modification of the target behavior to an acceptable criterion and significant overt efforts to change are the hallmarks of action.
5. *Maintenance*: Individuals work to prevent relapse and consolidate the gains attained during action. Stabilizing behavior change and avoiding relapse are the hallmarks of maintenance.

Source: James O. Prochaska, Carlo C. DiClemente, and John C. Norcross. "In Search of How People Change." *American Psychologist*. September 1992: 1102–1114. Copyright 1992 by the American Psychological Association. Reprinted by permission.

- Flexibility and alternative behavior
- Stress management
- Goal reinforcement[6]

Often, hospitalization for other concomitant problems provides an opportunity to begin smoking cessation. This is particularly true if the illness is related to or exacerbated by smoking. Frequently, smoke-free hospital environments provide counseling or support groups that the patient can participate in during recovery from the primary illness.[5]

Pharmacological Treatment

As in other addiction treatments, thus far there is no "magic bullet" that enables smokers to achieve abstinence instantly and sustain it for even one year. Smoking cessation is often a series of peaks and valleys in which, fortunately, smokers become more successful the more frequently they try. Smokers have a far more difficult time defeating the behavioral aspects of smoking and the "automatic" relapses than they do simply withdrawing or detoxifying from the drug. While there are anecdotal reports of methods used to reduce symptoms during detoxification (e.g., sucking on lollipops), there are few effective nonpharmacological treatments. Most of the current approaches are aimed at reducing withdrawal through controlled nicotine intake, maintenance stabilization, and detoxification. Most pharmacological treatments are initiated for detoxification but fail to focus on the behavioral change necessary for success or the identification and treatment of underlying or comorbid conditions such as depression or general anxiety. Nicotine replacement is an attempt to bridge the period between smoking, recognizing smoking cues, receiving doctor-administered drugs versus self-administered drugs leading ultimately to detoxification, and cessation.

Nicotine Replacement.   The concept of nicotine replacement is simple: Nicotine use is better than tobacco's toxic effects. In a lesser-of-two-evils environment, this is not a difficult choice: preventing the inhalation of a toxic waste cloud on an hourly or minute-by-minute basis is where the most important intervention should occur. This is especially important to the practitioner who has to cope with multiple medical conditions that are exacerbated by smoking. Overall, a successful nicotine replacement program can lead to saving millions of lives.[16]

Nicotine replacement has become a viable option as we have come to understand the vast network of circuits and pathways that control the drive for reward and reinforcement. Over the past decade, animal studies with a variety of substances have demonstrated that part of the addictive process may be related as much to the method of administration as to the substance itself. Studies of animals self-stimulating versus stimulation on a control basis have shown that the self-stimulating animals will become addicted while the control stimulation animals receiving the same level of substance will not. Theoretically, then, physician-regulated nicotine delivery systems should control nicotine use.

Over the past two decades, nicotine replacement has become a popular treatment for smokers. Studies by Hughes and Hatsukami and Henningfield have examined the viability of nicotine replacement and detoxification as part of a smoking cessation program.[17,18] Nicotine chewing gum was the first generally available nicotine replacement system; however, absorption was impaired through oral and gastric side effects or concomitant use with coffee, tea, and other stimulants. In addition, lack of control simply transferred dependency from one substance to another. Soon after nicotine gum, transdermal patches, intranasal sprays, and inhalers came on the scene. Over the past several years, randomized trials of all of these systems and devices has strongly suggested that they are most effective aids to smoking cessation when used in combination with pharmacological treatment and other forms of therapy or support.

One of the key elements of nicotine replacement is its ability to thwart withdrawal symptoms, coupled with potentially breaking the toxic cycle smokers are caught in.

When part of a comprehensive treatment plan, nicotine replacement can double long-term abstinence rates. While seemingly contradictory, nicotine replacement can be appropriate for those who are pregnant or have a history of heart disease, solely because it will prevent tobacco use, which is far more detrimental. Obviously, a complete history and documentation of all concomitant conditions should be initiated prior to initiation of nicotine.[5]

Several nicotine replacement options are available.

Nicotine Polacrilex (Gum).   Nicotine gum slows delivery of the effects of nicotine to the brain. It may take 7–10 seconds for a puff of smoke to reach the brain. Nicotine gum takes 15–30 minutes to have the same effect.[11]

Unfortunately, there have been mixed results associated with nicotine polacrilex, especially if not used with an overall intervention program. Improper use and noncompliance have been cited as reasons for treatment failure with this product. For a gum to be effective, blood levels would need to be comparable to those of a smoker and sustainable. Even with more nicotine added to the standard gum, this would be difficult to achieve. It would appear that nicotine polacrilex's best role may be as an adjunct to transdermal patch treatment or as part of a long-range program after the acute phase of abstinence is complete.

Nicotine Patch.   Initially the transdermal nicotine patch gave great hope to smokers who wanted to stop. And, in fact, there have been long-term success rates of 20%–30% reported when the patch is part of an overall program.[12] In addition, it is the best first-line therapy for the management of withdrawal symptoms. In general, the patch is best indicated for heavy smokers who reach for a cigarette before they reach for their toothbrush each morning.

To some extent, the dose is related to smoking levels, with the ratio being something along the lines of 1 mg to one cigarette. Thinner patients—below 100 pounds—should begin with a 21 or 22-mg patch. After a short period, the dose can be regulated. Initial side effects may include insomnia, skin rash, and itching. Studies report that limited skin irritations occur in between 20% and 50% of patients, and fewer than 10% of patients reporting reactions cease using the patch for this reason. Symptomatic treatment with hydrocortisone cream or another similar agent will generally reduce the reaction.[2] If bad dreams occur, which is possible, then the patch should be discontinued at night and reinitiated the next day.

Use of the patch while still smoking—which has been reported to cause nicotine poisoning, acute myocardial infarction, and other effects—is a problem to be addressed and indicates that clinical intervention and behavioral modification are not succeed

---

Main Reasons Why Nicotine Polacrilex Is Not Effective

- Physicians do not prescribe it correctly.[19]
- Smokers are afraid of nicotine or need extensive instruction in the proper use of the gum. Many chew it instead of keeping it in their cheeks.[20]
- Less than half of the 2 mg of nicotine in the gum is absorbed into the bloodstream.[21]
- Coffee and carbonated liquids can reduce absorption;[22] and results can depend upon whether the smoker has the gum or is provided gum at no cost.[23]
- The most serious problems appear to be prescribing gum to unmotivated patients,[24] underdosing,[25] and determining whether a difficult-to-use product which is a gum but not a chewing gum can be successful in general medical practice.[26]

---

ing. This is where the practitioner can intervene aggressively to assist in behavioral treatment or arrange a more intense program.

The initial, titrated dose should continue until patients have been abstinent for between two and four weeks. Any smoking at all during the first two weeks is a very poor prognostic sign. At that point, patients may be weaned to smaller doses.[5]

Currently, there are four different versions of the patch: three are worn around the clock, while the other is used only while awake or for 16 hours at a time. In general, we prefer the around-the-clock patch. Treatment should continue for two months; however, if the patient has not been able to stop most cigarette use within the first month of treatment, then the program is not working, and therapy should be reinitiated on a new date.[12]

Treatment Issues.   Many people on the patch complain that they fall off, especially in hot, humid climates where people sweat a great deal. Some patients put tape on the patch; others put it on areas where they sweat less. Sometimes a doctor will change the brand of patch to try to get better adhesion.

In general, from a clinical point of view, more than one patch may be given for those who smoke more than two packs per day.

Nicotine Patch Facts

- How long: 8–40 weeks
- Fiore's meta-analysis of the patch to be published in *JAMA*: 17 studies included on 5000 patients on patch with 50% on placebo patch. Mean levels of abstinence in all patch studies, effective rate at 6 months 22% versus 9% with placebo patch.
- The 16-hour patch will be withdrawn from the market but the 24-hour patch had no differences.
- 8-week treatment was equivalent to treating for more than 8 weeks.
- Group counseling and more intense counseling improved efficacy of the patch.
- Patch is efficacious but the absolute abstinence rate is highly dependent on counseling.
- Basic length of treatment should be six to eight weeks Habitrol or Nicoderm two to four weeks 21 mg, two weeks on 14 mg followed by two weeks on 7 mg.
  Criteria for use on patch: motivated to quit, 20 or more cigarettes per day, strong urges to smoke or smoke within 30 minutes of awakening. Since most smokers have tried to stop on their own, they should be evaluated and treated with the patch.

Source: Michael Fiore, M.D., a tobacco specialist and internist at the University of Wisconsin, 25th Conference of the American Society of Addiction Medicine, April 14–17, 1994, New York, New York.

A highly motivated pregnant woman can be given the patch as long as the benefit from the use of the patch outweighs the risks of smoking.

Medical-legal problems are always possible in the pregnant smoker, and the patch should be reserved for repeat failures.

If the patient has higher levels of nicotine or cotinine when smoking and has less on the patch, it is logical to assume that the pregnant woman is at no greater risk.

Breast milk is not generally a problem because of the relatively poor oral absorption of nicotine.

Clonidine. Clonidine is an antihypertensive medication used to treat opiate withdrawal. It appears to decrease release of nor-epinephrine as a result of its effects at the pontine nucleus and the locus coeruleus. With smokers, it appears to reduce the craving, irritability, impatience, anxiety, and restlessness associated with nicotine withdrawal.

Although clonidine has been effective in hypertension and also in opiate, benzodiazepine, and alcohol withdrawal, it may not be as effective with nicotine withdrawal, since opioid withdrawal symptoms encompass excessively rapid heart rate, dilated pupils, hypertension, hyperalertness, and decreased appetite. In nicotine withdrawal, however, there is diminished sympathetic activity with decreased heart rate, drowsiness, and increased appetite. The common denominator that clonidine affects may be the increased levels of anxiety for opiate users and smokers.[11]

Some disadvantages include its use in hypotensive patients, compliance problems, inconsistent blood levels, and side effects, including orthostatic symptoms, fatigue, dry mouth, and seda-tion.[6,29]

Further trials on specific populations—men versus women—may show that clonidine is more effective in reducing cravings in women than in men.[7]

Anxiolytics. Most smokers report anxiety during smoking cessation. Most anxiolytics have been studied with mixed results. Buspirone, among others, has shown some success in relief of anxiety but has not reduced withdrawal symptoms. Its anti-depressant properties may contribute to its effect in certain popu-lations with underlying depression who report only symptoms of anxiety.[11]

Antidepressants. Similarly, several selective serotonin reup-take inhibitors (SSRI) antidepressants with serotonergic effects are being studied with some success. It's hoped that these agents will prevent dysthymia, depression, and anger associated with smok-ing cessation.[7]

Nicotine Nasal Spray

Nicotine nasal sprays work faster than gum or the patch and the effects are somewhat similar to smoking inhalation. The rapid delivery system in a self-administered system can help ward off relapse and withdrawal symptoms. There are some early reports of success with the nasal spray. One study[11,27] reported 65% success at two weeks and 30% success at one year, with abstinence chemically validated.[11,28]

Recent studies of fluoxetine have also been promising, especially in reducing obsessive-compulsive thinking about cigarettes and weight gain. As a long-acting 5HT reuptake inhibitor, fluoxetine works very well in treating depression[11] and appears useful in patients who have had numerous failures at abstinence and those with prominent withdrawal dysphoria or concurrent underlying depression. As has been stated before, smokers with a history of depression indicate that they are more withdrawal-sensitive than those without a history of depression. A study conducted by Dalack and Glassman indicates that this particular group of smokers can be treated effectively with fluoxetine.

Other antidepressants such as the DA-augmenting bupropion also hold some promise in helping smokers stop. According to Linda H. Ferry, "The remarkable long-term success in these subjects is greater than with any previously reported pharmacologic agent for cessation. The drug works best in patients who aren't depressed."[30]

In one study, veterans who smoked one pack a day and were treated with bupropion reported a clear reduction of craving for cigarettes over the first month to month and half of use. Although about one-third reported some side effects such as dry mouth, the positive results have encouraged other similar studies of other populations.[30]

Nicotine Fading

Obviously, total cessation is often not possible, so a program of "fading" can be initiated, using both nicotine gum and the patch. Nicotine fading requires setting a stop date—one's anniversary, for example—and gradually reducing the amount of nicotine intake before the stop date. Most people who stop smoking for the first time choose this method. However, it should be tried in conjunction with counseling and education. Smokers are asked to keep a record of the time each cigarette is smoked. Another type of nicotine fading is to smoke a nonpreferred brand (an aversion stimulus), resulting in the smoker's smoking less and thereby ingesting less nicotine.

Used in fading, nicotine gum is prescribed only after the patient completely understands how to use the polacrilex. Nicotine polacrilex is not chewed like bubble gum; instead, it is gently chewed as one would puff on a cigarette and then parked between the teeth and the cheek and absorbed across the buccal mucosa. A gum-fading schedule is planned after the daily maintenance dose is established. Patients must be reminded not to smoke while using polacrilex.

Source: J.A. Cocores. The Clinical Management of Nicotine Addiction. In N.S. Miller, ed., *Comprehensive Handbook of Drug and Alcohol Addiction*. New York: Marcel Dekker, 1993.

Experimental Treatments. Experimental treatments are under way at many sites. Among them is a study of mecalamine, which blocks the nicotinic receptors in the acetylcholine receptor channel. It's been suggested that nicotine antagonists can help reduce the reward response provoked by nicotine. In this case, use of mecalamine may be thwarted by lack of patient compliance, since this drug can have multiple side effects and the withdrawal phase may be more intense than normal.[11]

Similarly, studies of propranolol have looked at whether or not beta blockers can be effective in controlling the reward mechanism of nicotine. Thus far, these studies have been inconclusive.[11]

How Smoking May Interfere with Drug Therapy

Research shows that in many instances smoking can interfere with drug therapy. This chart lists commonly prescribed drugs and the effects a patient's smoking can have on the drug's efficacy.

Drug	*The Effect Smoking Has on Drug Therapy*
Acetaminophen	The efficacy of this drug is not markedly affected by smoking. However, since plasma levels are lower in smokers, some patients may require higher doses than others.
Antidepressants (tricyclic)	Higher-than-normal doses may be needed since plasma levels are lower in smokers.
Benzodiazepines	These drugs are more rapidly eliminated by smokers, so that sedation is reduced. The effect is proportional to the amount of smoking—heavy smokers may need higher doses.
Caffeine	Smoking enhances caffeine elimination. Smokers generally experience less CNS stimulation from caffeine than do nonsmokers.
Cyanocobalamin (Vitamin B_{12})	Smoking lowers B_{12} levels. This can be particularly important in dealing with malnourished patients.
Glutethimide (Doriden, etc.)	Smoking appears to either lessen the volume of distribution or increase the fraction of drug absorbed, thus enhancing CNS depression.

In addition, some investigators have examined whether or not the release of endorphins is connected to this reinforcement response. If this is so, then cravings could be reduced by using naltrexone and naloxone,[11] which are beta-endorphin antagonists. Naltrexone has been shown to reduce opioid and also alcohol relapses in addicts, though these were previously thought to be apples and oranges.

Lidocaine HCl (Xylo- caine HCl, etc.)	An increase of about 20% in serum protein bind- ing has been observed in smokers—the clinical significance is unclear.
Oral contraceptives	The risk of thromboembolic events for those who use oral contraceptives increases with more than 15 cigarettes a day, especially after age 35.
Pentazocine HCl	Smoking greatly enhances metabolism. Increased maintenance doses may be needed if the initial dose is not affected.
Phenothiazines	Decreased effect of the drugs has been reported for smokers.
Phenylbutazone (Azolid, Buta- zolidin, etc.)	Smoking nearly doubles metabolic clearance. Higher doses may be needed by smokers.
Propoxyphene HCl (Darvon, SK-65, etc.)	Decreased efficacy is reported in smokers—this may be due to enhanced metabolism.
Propranolol HCl (Inderal)	Reports of increased clearance and reduced ther- apeutic effect in smokers continue to appear. Propranolol and smoking both impair periph- eral circulation, and smoking may negate the beneficial effects of propranolol in ischemic heart disease.
Theophylline	Half-life is decreased in smokers because of ac- celerated metabolism.

Source: A.G. Lipman. "How Smoking Interferes with Drug Therapy." *Modern Medicine*, August 1985, 141–142.

ACTH. In animal studies it has been repeatedly found that chronic nicotine administration keeps weight down and that nicotine-treated animals gain more weight than controls after discontinuation of the drug. It is striking to compare the symptoms of hypoglycemia—tremor, sweating, increased irritability, cognitive performance difficulties, headache, palpitations, and weakness—with what is sometimes seen with nicotine withdrawal. It can be hypothesized that ingesting large amounts of high-carbohydrate-containing food may be a form of self-medication to keep withdrawal more under control. Studies also indicate that increased intake of carbohydrates may lead directly to increased demand for endorphin release, which, in turn, creates a cycle that produces craving for more carbohydrates. Ture Arvidsson, Stockholm, Sweden, has for several decades been using ACTH on symptoms with intensive cognitive dysfunction like loss of creativity, inability to concentrate, and so on.

Hypnosis. Hypnotherapy has been used successfully in between 20% and 50% of those who have tried it, with some degree of success in maintaining abstinence. The success rate seems to depend on who is reporting the study. There are very few data, and hypnosis should be used only after other therapies are tried and/or as part of an overall treatment program.[6]

Acupuncture. Ear acupuncture has reduced symptoms of nicotine withdrawal, including craving, restlessness, and anxiety, in some patients. Acupuncture may also alleviate weight gain. Like hypnosis, acupuncture is still relatively untested and should not be used as a stand-alone effort.[6]

Scopolamine. Scopolamine has been used to alleviate withdrawal symptoms but is most frequently used to combat motion sickness, generally in a transcutaneous patch and as part of a recovery program. Applied to the mastoid area, transcutaneous scopolamine is not recommended for use beyond six days and is contraindicated in patients with a known hypersensitivity to scopolamine.[6]

There are a few over-the-counter products that are frequently tried by smokers. These include silver acetate lozenges, which are supposed to provoke a bitter taste when used with cigarettes. These lozenges can be helpful in an overall program.[6,11] Lobeline, a weak nicotinic receptor agonist, has been tried as a nicotine re-

---

Low-Tar and Low-Nicotine Cigarettes: Less Is More!

Are low-tar and low-nicotine cigarettes healthier? Smokers believe that "light" cigarettes are less dangerous, but the evidence, according to the *New York Times*, is quite the opposite.

Tar and nicotine levels are currently measured by the tobacco companies in their laboratories under Federal Trade Commission supervision, via a "smoking machine," but the results bear little resemblance to the results in actual smokers.

According to Matthew L. Meyers, a lawyer for an antismoking group representing the American Heart Association, the Lung Association, and the Cancer Society, "The FTC method is so flawed that it raises a serious question whether the method causes more harm than good. . . . In addition, the tiny filtration holes are often blocked by smokers with their lips or hands, thus cutting off the air that would have diluted the smoke."

Source: Philip Hilts. "Major Flaw Cited in Cigarette Data." *New York Times*, May 1, 1994.

---

placement agent, but with little success and little evidence that it can be useful in smoking cessation.[9,31,32]

Along with nicotine antagonists, weight reduction agents such as phenylpropanolamine[33] or dexfenfluramine are often used. As mentioned previously, weight gain can be minimized through exercise and behavioral modification, and diet programs used with smoke ending can be a "double whammy" for the smoker. It's best to concentrate on smoking reduction and let the weight reduction program follow after withdrawal is complete.[33]

Reduced-Tar Cigarettes. Reduced-tar cigarettes have been marketed from time to time, although the concept is somewhat ironic considering that the tobacco industry feels that smoking is not harmful. The bottom line with no-tar cigarettes is simple: smokers don't like them because they don't taste as good as

---

California Smoke Helpline

Cigarette tax money in California, Proposition 99, have provided clinicians with funding for a variety of innovative programs. Among the most innovative, is the statewide California Smoking Helpline of the University of California. According to its director, psychologist S. Zhu, the program attempts to improve upon the existing dismal success rate in tobacco treatment.

Approximately 25,000 people have had counseling over the phone from the California Smoke Helpline. This type of counseling helps people who cannot get to a counseling appointment, who have transportation or child care problems, or who are Spanish-speaking. Dr. Zhu's 800 number screens patients on the basis of one question: "Are you ready to quit?" A respondent who answers "No" is sent a book with information on how to stop smoking on one's own. However, 65% say yes, they want counseling.

The hotline provides a counselor who calls the client (counselor-initiated) at a specific time and date. All follow-up counseling occurs when the counselor calls. The counselor is a clinician who follows a treatment protocol so that the first session is 45–60 minutes long and the remainder are 20 minutes long.

Counseling is front-end-loaded to respond to the high probability of relapse early in treatment.

The counselor–client relationship provides convenience and anonymity, making treatment quicker for many patients, since the smoker has the

---

regular cigarettes and they have to change their "puffing" behavior to achieve similar nicotine yield. The studies of low-tar cigarettes show that nicotine intake is reduced—often by as much as 44%—however, carbon monoxide intake increases.[34,35]

Relapse Prevention

The smoking relapse rate after initial abstinence is very similar to that of alcohol and other addicting drugs. Patients should be taught to anticipate relapse situations and what to do if that situation arises. If relapse does occur, the event that led to the ability to imagine the counselor in a variety of ways. The counselor tries to call when he or she expects extreme urges or the likelihood of relapse. Such a model is easily applicable to the office setting, where telephone counseling can be a cost-effective alternative to setting up an appointment, which the patient most likely will not keep.

While hearing and supporting the client through the difficulties of quitting, the counselor must focus on the self-image and perception of success. Coping strategies are both defensive ("What do you do at a party where people are smoking?") and offensive, helping the client to visualize and think about what a nonsmoker does at a party and how nonsmokers cope with stress and conflict. The smoker's motivation needs a boost and the counselor provides reinforcement and support. Smokers are asked to list the situations where they think they would be at most risk of relapse.

With more counseling, smokers feel more competent to stop. Even for the most addicted, counseling still had an important effect and may be an important addition to treatment with a nicotine patch.

Patients who relapse tend to relapse in an emotional situation or conflict rather than simply in response to extreme withdrawal or craving. The most motivated patients are the most successful, but most patients slip or relapse many times before successfully stopping. Those patients with the most environmental and social stigma, like those with a recent catastrophic illness, appear to do better regardless of treatment type.

Source: 25th Conference of the American Society of Addiction Medicine, April 13–17, 1994, New York, New York.

relapse should be reviewed, and changes should be made to prevent or more effectively deal with the circumstances in the future. The patient should then be encouraged to set another stop date and try again. Telephone counseling has been shown to help maintain abstinence and prevent relapse. Frequent follow-up visits, especially when effective counseling is provided, can help prevent relapse. Other types of contact, such as a series of letters, can maintain contact with the patient and emphasize the importance of continued abstinence.[12]

Relapse is a part of the definition of addiction, and therefore the tobacco user is just as likely to relapse as the cocaine or heroin

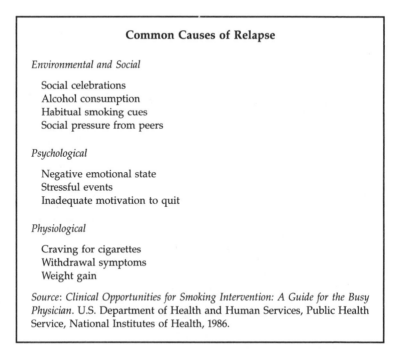

Common Causes of Relapse

Environmental and Social

    Social celebrations
    Alcohol consumption
    Habitual smoking cues
    Social pressure from peers

Psychological

    Negative emotional state
    Stressful events
    Inadequate motivation to quit

Physiological

    Craving for cigarettes
    Withdrawal symptoms
    Weight gain

Source: *Clinical Opportunities for Smoking Intervention: A Guide for the Busy Physician*. U.S. Department of Health and Human Services, Public Health Service, National Institutes of Health, 1986.

user. The practitioner must explain to the patient that relapse is not failure; it is simply another start. It's important to make sure that all treatment programs have good relapse prevention and "start-over programs."

Guidelines for relapse prevention include:

1. Using all energy and determination to avoid nicotine.
2. Planning ahead for hazards and temptations.
3. Breaking the pattern of stimulus and response.
4. Restoring and strengthening the body through diet and exercise.
5. Finding alternative interests and pleasures.
6. Learning to handle anxiety and depression.

Seven Steps to Prevent Relapse

1. Remind patients at each office visit of the clinical consequences of smoking.
2. Provide positive reinforcement emphasizing the benefits of quitting.
3. Provide take-home materials that encourage maintenance of cessation.
4. Refer patients to community maintenance programs or ex-smokers' hotlines.
5. Emphasize that repeated cessation attempts are often necessary for success.
6. Prepare patients for the short-term results of cessation—both possible withdrawal symptoms and immediate benefits (e.g., better breath, better ability to taste).
7. Follow up with patients between office visits by telephone or mail.

Source: *Clinical Opportunities for Smoking Intervention: A Guide for the Busy Physician*. U.S. Department of Health and Human Services, Public Health Service, National Institutes of Health, 1986.

---

7. Dealing with troubled relationships without nicotine.
8. Socializing with other recovering smokers.
9. Mentally reviewing prior relapses.

Relapsed smokers must know that they can start again and should also know that, once they do, their chances of maintaining abstinence increase with each new start. Motivation and commitment to quitting negate the relapse event.[6]

Recovery

When do you become a "recovered smoker"? Generally, a year of abstinence is considered "recovery." But since relapse is so common among smokers, there must be an awareness among both clinicians and smokers that they, like all other "addicts," are always "in recovery." The fact is that we don't really know much about the long-term potential for recovery of heavy nicotine addicts; however, 50% of those who ever smoked have stopped. With education and relapse prevention techniques, clinicians can help redefine this concept.[5]

References

1. Physician treatment of nicotine addiction. *The Facts about Tobacco, Alcohol and Other Drugs*, Vol. 3, No. 1, Winter 1994.
2. Smoking interventions: What you can do. *Clinical Opportunities for Smoking Intervention: A Guide for the Busy Physician*. U.S. Dept. of Health and Human Services, Public Health Service, National Institutes of Health, 1986.
3. Hearn W. Why don't smokers quit? *Am Med News*. December 27, 1993.
4. Glynn TJ, Manley MW. *How to Help Your Patients Stop Smoking: A National Cancer Institute Manual for Physicians*. Smoking and Tobacco Control Program, Division of Cancer Prevention and Control National Cancer Institute, 1992.
5. Slade J. Nicotine dependence: Intervention strategies for the physician. *NJ Med*. 1993;90(11):831–834.
6. Cocores JA. The clinical management of nicotine addiction. In Miller NS, ed., *Handbook of Drug and Alcohol Addiction*. New York: Marcel Dekker.
7. Fagerstrom KO. Toward better diagnoses and more individual treatment of tobacco dependence. *Br J Addiction*. 1991;86:543–547.
8. Hollis JF, Lichtenstein E, Vogt TM et al. Nurse-assisted counseling for smokers in primary care. *Ann Intern Med*. 1993;118(7):521–525.
9. Schwartz JL. Review and evaluation of smoking cessation methods: The United States and Canada, 1978–1985. U.S. Department of Health and Human Services. Public Health Services, National Institutes of Health. Washington, DC: Government Printing Office, 1987.
10. Mermelstein R, Cohen S, Lichtenstein E, et al. Social support and smoking cessation and maintenance. *J Consult Clin Psychol*. 1986; 54:447–453.
11. Jarvik ME, Schneider NA. Nicotine. In Lowinstein JH, Ruiz P, Millman RB, eds., *Substance Abuse: Comprehensive Textbook*. Baltimore: Williams & Wilkins, 1992.

12. Hurt RD. Nicotine dependence-treatment for the 1990s. Editorial. *J Intern Med*. 1993;233:307–310.
13. U.S. Department of Health and Human Services. *The Health Consequences of Smoking: A Report of the Surgeon General*. Washington DC: Government Printing Office, 1988.
14. Raw M. The treatment of cigarette dependence. In Isreal Y, Glaser FB, Kalant H, Popham RE, Schmidt W, Smart RG, eds., *Research Advances in Alcohol and Drug Problems*. New York: Plenum Press, 1978.
15. Carmody TP. Preventing relapse in the treatment of nicotine addiction: Current issues and future directions. *J Psychoactive Drugs*. 1990; 22(2):211–238.
16. Russell MA. The future of nicotine replacement. *Br J Addiction*. 1991;86:653–658.
17. Hughes JR, Hatsukami DK, Skoog KP. Physical dependence on nicotine in gum: A placebo substitution trial. *JAMA*. 1986;255:3277–3279.
18. Henningfield JE, Radzius A, Cooper TM et al. Drinking coffee and carbonated beverages blocks absorption of nicotine from nicotine polacrilex gum. *JAMA*. 1990;264:1560–1564.
19. Cummings S, Hansen B, Richard RJ et al. Internists and nicotine gum. *JAMA*. 1988;260:1565–1569
20. Schneider NG. Nicotine gum in smoking cessation: Rationale, efficacy, and proper use. *Compr Ther*. 1987;13:32–37.
21. Benowitz NL. Toxicity of nicotine: implications with regard to nicotine replacement therapy. In Pomerleau OF, Pomerleau CS, eds., *Nicotine Replacement: A Critical Evaluation*. New York: Liss, 1988.
22. Henningfield JE, London ED, Benowitz NL. Arterial-venous differences in plasma concentrations of nicotine after cigarette smoking. *JAMA*. 1990;263(15):2049–2050
23. Cox JL, McKenna JP. Nicotine gum: Does providing it free in smoking cessation program alter success rates? *J Fam Pract*. 1990;31(3):278–280.
24. Research Committee of the British Thoracic Society. Smoking cessation in patients: Two further studies by the British Thoracic Society. *Thorax*. 1990;45:835–840.
25. Schneider NG. *How to Use Nicotine Gum and Other Strategies to Quit Smoking*. New York: Simon & Schuster, 1988.
26. Hughes JR, Miller SA. Nicotine gum to help stop smoking. *JAMA*. 1984;2252:2855–2858.
27. Jarvis, M. Nasal nicotine solution: Its potential in smoking cessation

and as a research tool. In Ockene JK, ed., *The Pharmacologic Treatment of Tobacco Dependence: Proceedings of the World Congress.* Cambridge: Harvard Institute for the Study of Smoking Behavior and Policy, 1986.

28. Perkins KA, Grobe JE, Stilleer RL et al. Nasal spray nicotine replacement suppresses cigarette smoking desire and behavior. *Clin Pharmacol Therapeut.* 1992;52(6):627–634.

29. Ornish SA, Zisook S, McAdams LA. Effects of transdermal clonidine treatment on withdrawal symptoms associated with smoking cessation. *Arch Intern Med.* 1988;148:2027–2031.

30. Jancin, B. Bupropion can help recidivist smokers quit, research shows. *Clin Psychiatr News.* February 1993.

31. Gritz ER, Jarvik ME. Pharmacological aids for the cessation of smoking. In Steinfeld J, Griffitths W, Ball K, Taylor R, eds., *Proceedings of the 3rd World Conference on Smoking and Health.* Washington, DC: U.S. DHEW, Public Health Service, 1977.

32. Sachs DPI. Cigarette smoking health effects and cessation strategies. *Clin Geriatr Med.* 1986;2:337–362.

33. Spring B, Pingitore R, Kessler K. Strategies to minimize weight gain after smoking cessation: Psychological and pharmacological intervention with specific reference to dexfenfluramine. *Inter J Obesity.* 1992;16(Suppl.3):S19–S23.

34. Sutherland G, Russell MA, Stapleton JA et al. Glycerol particle cigarettes: A less harmful option for chronic smokers. *Thorax.* 1993;48: 385–387.

35. Kolonen S. *Low-Yield Cigarettes: Smoke Exposure and Puffing Behaviour.* Kuopio Finland: Kuopio University Publications, 1992.

Additional Sources

Prochaska J, DiClemente CC, Norcross JC. In search of how people change. *American Psychologist.* 1992:1102–1114.

Dalack GW, Glassman AH, Rivelli S et al. Mood, major depression, and fluoxetine response in cigarette smokers. Presented at New Research Poster Session at 145th Annual Meeting of the American Psychiatric Association, May 2–7, 1992.

7

A Model Cessation Program

Basic Guidelines from the National Cancer Institute

One of the best-known and clinically tested programs for the practicing physician has been produced by the National Cancer Institute (NCI). It is a comprehensive program, developed over five years along with multiple components to be used in schools, communities, and other venues.

The NCI recognized the pressing demands on medical staff in all settings and has devised a program that fits with those demands. The interventions that follow are brief and direct, permitting use with all patient populations. The NCI recognized that all patients will not stop smoking when first approached, and that many will relapse and require several attempts before becoming abstinent. For this reason this program is designed so that it can be used repeatedly until success is achieved.

The program is available with the complete manual that the following information is taken from, a lecture and slide program, patient information sheets that can be reproduced, and other recyclable materials. To obtain complete copies of this program, at no cost, contact the National Cancer Institute and ask for NCI's "Quit for Good" materials and NIH Publication No. 92-3064, revised September 1992, or call 1-800-4-CANCER.

Synopsis for Physicians: How to Help Your Patients Stop Smoking

1. Ask about smoking at every opportunity.
    a. "Do you smoke?"
    b. "How much?"
    c. "How soon after waking do you have your first cigarette?"
    d. "Are you interested in stopping smoking?"
    e. "Have you ever tried to stop before?" If so, "What happened?"
2. Advise all smokers to stop.
    a. State your advice clearly, for example: "As your physician, I must advise you to stop smoking now."
    b. Personalize the message to quit. Refer to the patient's clinical condition, smoking history, family history, personal interests, or social roles.
3. Assist the patient in stopping.
    a. Set a quit date. Help the patient pick a date within the next four weeks, acknowledging that no time is ideal.
    b. Provide self-help materials. The smoking-cessation coordinator or support staff member can review the materials with the patient if desired (call 1-800-4-CANCER for NCI's *Quit for Good* materials).
    c. Consider prescribing nicotine gum, especially for highly addicted patients (those who smoke one pack a day or more or who smoke their first cigarette within 30 minutes of waking).

     d. Consider signing a stop-smoking contract with the patient.

     e. If the patient is not willing to quit now:
- Provide motivating literature (call 1-800-4-CANCER for NCI's *Why Do You Smoke?* pamphlet).
- Ask again at the next visit.

4. Arrange follow-up visits.

     a. Set a follow-up visit within one or two weeks after the quit date.

     b. Have a member of the office staff call or write the patient within seven days after initial visit, reinforcing the decision to stop and reminding the patient of the quit date.

     c. At the first follow-up visit, ask about the patient's smoking status to provide support and help prevent relapse. Relapse is common; if it happens, encourage the patient to try again immediately.

     d. Set a second follow-up visit in one or two months. For patients who have relapsed, discuss the circumstance of the relapse and other special concerns.

Synopsis for Office Staff: How to Develop Office Procedures to Help Patients Stop Smoking

1. Select an office smoking-cessation coordinator who will be responsible for seeing that the office smoking-cessation program is carried out.

2. Create a smoke-free office:

     a. Select a date for the office to become smoke-free.

     b. Advise all staff and patients of this plan.

     c. Post no-smoking signs in all office areas.

     d. Remove ashtrays.

     e. Display nonsmoking materials and cessation information prominently.

    f. Eliminate all tobacco advertising from the waiting room.

3. Identify all patients who smoke.
   a. Ask all patients, "Do you smoke?" or "Are you still smoking?" at each visit.
   b. Prominently place a "Smoker" identifier on the charts of all smoking patients.
   c. Attach a permanent progress card to each patient's chart.

4. Review self-help materials (provided by either the physician or the coordinator) and nicotine gum use (if a prescription has been given) with each smoking patient.

5. Assist the physician in making follow-up visits.
   a. With each patient who has agreed to a quit date, schedule a follow-up visit one or two weeks after the quit date.
   b. Call or write the patient within seven days after the initial visit to reinforce the decision to quit.
   c. Schedule a second follow-up visit approximately one to two months after the first follow-up visit.

Step 1: Select an Office Smoking-Cessation Coordinator

To be successful, a smoking-cessation program must be easy for the physician and staff to adopt as part of their routine office procedures. The five steps of this program are designed to be integrated smoothly into a variety of practices.

The first step is to select one person, the "smoking-cessation coordinator," to be responsible for incorporating the other four steps into the day-to-day activities of your practice. The person should be a current member of the staff, because the coordinator's job requires only a little additional time. In most practices, the coordinator is a nurse. Although the coordinator will have primary responsibility, other staff members should be involved in helping the coordinator implement the program.

Responsibilities of the smoking-cessation coordinator are to

- Become familiar with this manual and the basic components of the program.
- Ensure that Steps 2–5 of the program are implemented.
- Maintain, along with the physician, the staff's commitment to the program as an integral part of the practice's day-to-day activities.

Step 2: Create a Smoke-Free Office

Fortunately, most physicians serve as nonsmoking role models for their patients. The physician's office should also convey a nonsmoking message and help set the stage for the advice and counseling to be provided to the patients. The activities in Step 2 can be conducted by the smoking cessation coordinator, with the assistance of other office staff and the encouragement and cooperation of the physician.

Select a date to make the office smoke free. Establishing an office no-smoking policy for both staff and patients is a necessary step in implementing this program. This action will emphasize your strong commitment to nonsmoking and to the health of your patients, including nonsmokers who are exposed to the smoke of others. At this stage and at every step of this program, it is helpful to maintain an empathetic relationship with patients who smoke, while providing all the assistance you can to help them stop. The date you set should leave adequate time to prepare your staff and patients for the new policy, as discussed below.

Advise all staff and patients of this plan. Once you have set a date for your office to become smoke free, it is important to inform staff and patients of your plans. A period of 4–6 weeks should provide enough time for you to introduce this policy without losing the momentum begun by setting the date. You may want to send patients a note, which can also be handed out during office visits and posted in the office. An example of this kind of note follows.

Introduction of a Smoke-Free Policy in This Office

The Surgeon General of the United States has declared that
cigarette smoking is the chief, single, avoidable cause of
death in our society and the most important public health
issue of our time. Recognizing the health problems associated
with cigarette smoking, for both smokers and those around
them, this office will become smoke free on _____. After that
time, a no-smoking policy for patients and staff will be
adopted within this office. We realize that this may be difficult for some of you, and encourage you to ask our smoking
cessation coordinator, _____, about information and advice
we can provide to you about stopping smoking. We will all be
healthier for this action, and we thank you for your cooperation.

Larger institutions may need to take additional steps before
adopting a smoke-free policy.

Step 2: Action Summary

1. Select a date to make the office smoke free.
2. Advise all staff and patients of this plan.
3. Post no-smoking signs in all office areas.
4. Remove ashtrays from all office areas.
5. Prominently display smoking cessation materials and information.
6. Eliminate all tobacco advertising from the waiting room.

Step 3: Action Summary

1. Assess the smoking status of all patients in the practice
while measuring vital signs; smokers should complete the brief
Patient Smoking Assessment Form.

2. Prominently place a "Smoker" identifier on the chart of
all smoking patients; consider placing a removable "Did You
Counsel about Smoking?" sticker on the charts of smoking pa-

tients at each visit to remind the physician to address smoking with these patients.

3. Use a permanent progress card (e.g., the Patient Smoking Assessment Form) for each smoking patient. Attach the card to the patient's chart for the physician to complete and the smoking-cessation coordinator to review at each visit.

Step 4: Action Summary

1. Ask about smoking at every opportunity.
2. Advise all smokers to stop.
3. Assist the patient in stopping.
   a. Help set a quit date.
   b. Provide self-help materials.
   c. Consider a stop-smoking contract with the patient.
4. Arrange follow-up visits (see Step 5).

Step 5: Action Summary

1. Arrange a follow-up visit within one or two weeks after the patient's quit date.
2. Within seven days of the first visit, call or send a letter to the patient reinforcing the decision to stop and providing a reminder of the quit date.
3. At the first follow-up visit, ask about the patient's smoking status and discuss progress and problems.
4. Arrange a second follow-up visit in one to two months.

Responses to Patients' Common Questions and Concerns

1. Won't I gain weight if I stop smoking?
   • Not every person who stops smoking gains weight.

- Average weight gains are small for people who do gain (5–10 lbs).
- Don't diet now—there will be time after you are an established nonsmoker.
- Exercise is an effective technique to cope with withdrawal and to avoid weight gain.
- Avoid high-calorie snacks. Vegetables (such as carrot sticks) and fruits are good snacks.
- The risks to health from smoking are far greater than the risks to health from a small weight gain.
- A small increase in weight may not hurt your appearance. Smoking is unattractive, causing yellow teeth, bad breath, stale clothing odors, and, possibly, wrinkled skin.

2. I don't have the willpower to stop smoking.
   - More than 3 million Americans stop smoking every year.
   - Not everyone succeeds the first time, but many people are successful after several attempts.
   - There are a variety of tips to help you in the written materials I will give you.
   - I will give you all the support I can.

3. I smoke only low-tar/low-nicotine cigarettes, so I don't need to stop.
   - There is no such thing as a safe cigarette.
   - Many smokers inhale more often or more deeply to compensate for low nicotine levels in these cigarettes.

4. Is it better to stop "cold turkey" or over a long period of time?
   - There is no "best way."
   - Most successful former smokers quit "cold turkey."

5. What about insomnia?
   Many smokers report having problems sleeping after they stop smoking. If these symptoms are related to nicotine dependence, they should disappear within two to three weeks.

6. Why do I cough more now that I've stopped?
   About 20% of former smokers report an increase in coughing after they stop smoking. This is a temporary response thought to be caused by an increase in the lung's ability to remove phlegm, so it actually represents recovery of the lung's defense mechanisms.
7. Now that I've stopped, can I smoke a cigarette occasionally?
   No. Nicotine addiction seems to be retriggered quickly in most former smokers. Don't risk getting hooked again.
8. Will my body recover from the effects of smoking?
   - Some of the damage may be permanent, such as loss of lung tissue in emphysema.
   - Other functions are recovered, such as the lung's ability to remove phlegm.
   - The increased risk of heart disease due to smoking disappears in less than 10 years after stopping.
   - The increased risk of lung cancer disappears within 15 years.
9. I'd like to stop in a group setting. Where can I find a cessation program?
   - Call the American Cancer Society, the American Lung Association, or local hospitals.
   - Most people stop without the help of a formal group. Call the National Cancer Institute's Cancer Information Service toll free at 1-800-4-CANCER for suggestions about stop-smoking programs in your area. Trained counselors are also available at this number to answer questions about stopping and to provide written materials.
10. Should I tell other people I'm trying to stop?
    Yes. Patients should enlist the support of family, friends, and co-workers.
11. What should I do when I get an urge to smoke?
    - Some people relieve cravings by chewing gum, sucking on a cinnamon stick, or eating a carrot stick.

- Cravings for cigarettes are a normal part of withdrawal.
- Most cravings last for only a few minutes and then subside.
- Cravings become rare after a few weeks.
- Use nicotine gum, if prescribed.
12. When I don't smoke, I feel restless, and I can't concentrate.
    - These are normal symptoms of nicotine withdrawal.
    - These symptoms are most acute in the first three days after stopping.
    - These symptoms will disappear after a few weeks.
13. What other withdrawal symptoms will I have?
    - Some smokers have few or no withdrawal symptoms.
    - Other common symptoms include anxiety, irritability, mild headache, and gastrointestinal symptoms such as constipation.
    - Few smokers experience all these symptoms.
    - Like other symptoms, they are only temporary.

Selected Self-Help Smoking-Cessation Materials

This resource listing provides names and addresses of some of the organizations that have developed materials related to motivation, cessation, and maintenance. Also included are materials on smokeless tobacco and videotaped products. Inclusion of organizations or materials in this listing does not imply an endorsement of either the organization or its materials. Furthermore, the availability of material is subject to change. To identify new or updated materials, contact your local library or the organizations whose materials are cited in this listing.

AMERICAN CANCER SOCIETY
1599 Clifton Road, N.E.
Atlanta, GA 30329
404-320-3333

Danger: Cigarettes
Don't Bite Off More Than You Should Chew
How Can We Reach You? (for women)
How to Stay Quit over the Holidays
I'm In Charge Now . . . What's My Secret? (for women)
The Fifty Most Often Asked Questions about Smoking and
  Health and the Answers
Why Start Life under a Cloud? (for pregnant women)
Smart Move
Quitter's Guide 7 Day Plan to Help You Stop Smoking
  Cigarettes

AMERICAN COLLEGE OF OBSTETRICIANS AND GYNECOLOGISTS
ACOG Distribution Center
Suite 300 East
600 Maryland Avenue, S.W.
Washington, DC 20024-2588

Smoking and Women

AMERICAN DENTAL ASSOCIATION
211 East Chicago Avenue
Chicago, IL 60611
312-440-2500

Smokeless Tobacco
38 Million People Have Quit Smoking. You Can Too.

AMERICAN HEART ASSOCIATION
7320 Greenville Avenue
Dallas, TX 75231
214-822-9380

Calling It Quits
Guidelines for a Weight Control Component in a Smoking
  Cessation Program

AMERICAN LUNG ASSOCIATION
1740 Broadway
New York, NY 10019
212-315-8700

> A Healthy Beginning: The Smoke-Free Family Guide for
>   New Parents (kit)
> A Lifetime of Freedom from Smoking: A Maintenance Pro-
>   gram for Ex-Smokers
> Because You Love Your Baby
> Freedom from Smoking for You and Your Family
> Freedom from Smoking for You and Your Baby (kit)
> Freedom from Smoking in 20 Days
> In Control: A Home Video Freedom from Smoking Program
> Smokeless Tobacco: No Way
> Stop Smoking, Stay Trim

BLOOMINGTON HEART AND HEALTH PROGRAM
1900 West Old Shakopee Road
Bloomington, MN 55431
612-887-9603
612-887-9684 FAX

> Quit and Win

FOX CHASE CANCER CENTER
510 Township Line Road
Cheltenham, PA 19012
215-728-2794

> Clear Horizons (for older smokers)
> Stop Now for Your Baby
> Quitting Times (for women)

GROUP HEALTH COOPERATIVE OF PUGET SOUND
521 Wall Street
Seattle, WA 98121
1-800-437-6668

> Free and Clear

HEALTH PROMOTION RESOURCE CENTER
Stanford Center for Research in Disease Prevention
1000 Welch Road
Palo Alto, CA 304-1885
415-723-1000
415-723-0003

Calling It Quits (videotape)
Cool Turkey Quitting Guide: A Day-by-Day Program
to Help You Quit Smoking
Como Dejar de Fumar en Tres Pasos
Quit Smoking Kit

NATIONAL CANCER INSTITUTE
Office of Cancer Communications
Building 31, Room 10A24
Bethesda, MD 20892
1-800-4-CANCER

Chew or Snuff Is Real Bad Stuff
Clearing the Air—How to Quit Smoking and Quit for Keeps
Guia Para Dejar de Fumar
Why Do You Smoke?

NORTH CAROLINA MUTUAL LIFE INSURANCE COMPANY
411 West Chapel Hill Street
Durham, NC 27701
919-682-9201, Ext. 316

Quit for Life (kit for Black Americans)

OFFICE ON SMOKING AND HEALTH
Centers for Disease Control
1600 Clifton Road, N.E.
Mailstop K50
Atlanta, GA 30333
404-488-5705

Pregnant? That's Two Good Reasons to Quit Smoking
Is Your Baby Smoking?

UNIVERSITY OF CALIFORNIA SCHOOL OF MEDICINE
Division of General Internal Medicine
Room A-405
400 Parnassus Avenue
San Francisco, CA 94143-0320

  Quit for Life

Materials for Physicians and Office Staff

AMERICAN ACADEMY OF FAMILY PHYSICIANS
Health Education Department
8880 Ward Parkway
Kansas City, MO 64114-3246

  AAFP Stop Smoking Kit
  Family Physician's Guide to Smoking Cessation

AMERICAN CANCER SOCIETY
1599 Clifton Road, N.E.
Atlanta, GA 30329
404-320-3333

  Tobacco-Free Young America: A Kit for the Busy Practitioner

AMERICAN HOSPITAL ASSOCIATION
Order Services
840 N. Lakeshore Drive
Chicago, IL, 60611
312-280-0000

  Smoking and Hospitals Are a Bad Match

AMERICAN LUNG ASSOCIATION
1740 Broadway
New York, NY 10019
212-315-8700

A Healthy Beginning Counseling Kit

CENTER FOR CORPORATE PUBLIC INVOLVEMENT
1001 Pennsylvania Avenue, N.W.
Washington, DC 20004-2599

Nonsmoking in the Workplace—A Guide for Employers

MINNESOTA COALITION FOR A SMOKE-FREE SOCIETY 2000
Suite 400
2221 University Avenue, S.E.
Minneapolis, MN 55414
612-378-0902

Clean Air Health Care—A Guide To Establish Smoke-Free
Health Care Facilities

National Cancer Institute
Office of Cancer Communications
Building 31, Room 10A24
Bethesda, MD 20892
1-800-4-CANCER

How To Help Your Patients Stop Using Tobacco: A Na-
tional Cancer Institute Manual for the Oral Health Team
Self-Guided Strategies for Smoking Cessation: A Program
Planner's Guide
Quit for Good: A Practitioner's Stop-Smoking Guide (kit)
School Programs to Prevent Smoking: A Guide to Strate-
gies That Succeed

NATIONAL HEART, LUNG, AND BLOOD INSTITUTE
NHLBI Information Center
4733 Bethesda Avenue, Suite 530
Bethesda, MD 20814
(301) 951-3260

Clinical Opportunities for Smoking Intervention—A
Guide for the Busy Physician
How You Can Help Patients Stop Smoking: Opportunities
for Respiratory Care Practitioners
The Physician's Guide—How to Help Your Hypertensive
Patient Stop Smoking
Nurses: Help Your Patients Stop Smoking

OFFICE ON SMOKING AND HEALTH
Centers for Disease Control
1600 Clifton Road, N.E.
Mailstop K50
Atlanta, Ga 30333
404-488-5705

A Physician Talks about Smoking

Other Sources of Information

AMERICAN MEDICAL ASSOCIATION
Division of Communications
535 North Dearborn Street
Chicago, IL 60610
312-645-4419

DOCTORS OUGHT TO CARE (DOC)
HH-101
Medical College of Georgia
Atlanta, GA 30912
404-721-2739

STOP TEENAGE ADDICTION TO TOBACCO
P.O. Box 60658
Longmeadow, MA 01116
413-567-2070

8

Smoking and Special Populations

Children and Adolescents

Year after year, the health care profession fights disease and promotes health care improvement for our generation and generations to come. Yet in America today, cigarette use by children and adolescents remains one of the most serious health care problems we face—not only for its acute effects, but for its chronic effects. Every day, 3000 children light up cigarettes for the first time; 25% of that group will die prematurely because of smoking. And this activity is the beginning of a lifelong road to poor health, since 60% of all current smokers began by age 14.

Tobacco use is also connected to other problems that teenagers encounter. There is a wide-ranging body of literature that confirms that those who use other drugs of abuse rarely do so before they smoke. Adolescent tobacco users are substantially more likely to use alcohol and illegal drugs than are nonusers. As they move from one risk group to another, they will be more likely to engage in violent activity, use guns, try to kill themselves, and have high-risk sexual encounters. This behavior is not isolated

and can be considered part of overall negative behavioral syndromes that build upon each other.

Recent U.S. government studies show:

- 43% of male high school seniors who used smokeless tobacco also smoked cigarettes.
- Female and male adolescents are now equally likely to
  smoke. Male adolescents are substantially more likely than
  females to use smokeless tobacco products; about 20% of
  high school males report current use.
- White adolescents are more likely to smoke and to use
  smokeless tobacco than are black and Hispanic adolescents.
- Four different studies—National Household Surveys on
  Drug Abuse (NHSDA), Teenage Attitudes and Practices
  Survey (TAPS), Monitoring the Future Project (MTFP), and
  Youth Risk Behavior Survey (YRBS)—show "that by age 18,
  about two-thirds of adolescents in the United States have
  tried smoking. These surveys also show that the prevalence
  of ever smoking is greater among males than females. Ever
  smoking increased as a function of increasing age or grade
  in all 4 surveys. Adolescents living in the north-central
  region of the U.S. were the most likely to report having
  smoked."[1]

The Role of the Health Profession
in Preventing Smoking among the Young

Only recently, as the public's concern for the overall public
health problem caused by smoking has risen, have we seriously
examined use among children and adolescents. In fact, there have
been 23 reports on tobacco issued by the Surgeon General's office
since 1964, and it was not until recently that the former Surgeon
General, M. Joycelyn Elders, issued a report specifically about
tobacco use and young people.

It is late in the game for health care practitioners to be focusing on smoking; while smoking rates have declined somewhat in the adult population, onset rates among our youth have not. According to the Surgeon General, "28% of the nation's high school seniors are currently cigarette smokers," (Figure 8.1).

According to the Assistant Secretary for Health, Phillip R. Lee, M.D., and David Satcher, M.D., Ph.D, Director of the Centers for Disease Control Prevention:

> The onset of tobacco use occurs primarily in early adolescence, a developmental stage that is several decades removed from the death and disability that are associated with smoking and smokeless tobacco use in adulthood. Currently, very few people begin to use tobacco as adults, almost all first use

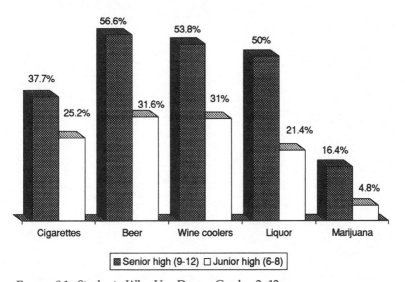

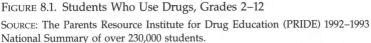

FIGURE 8.1. Students Who Use Drugs, Grades 2–12

SOURCE: The Parents Resource Institute for Drug Education (PRIDE) 1992–1993 National Summary of over 230,000 students.

has occurred by the time people graduate from high school. The earlier young people begin using tobacco, the more heavily they are likely to use it as adults, and the longer potential time they have to be users. Both the duration and the amount of tobacco use are related to eventual chronic health problems. The processes of nicotine addiction further ensure that many of today's adolescent smokers will regularly use tobacco when they are adults.

While it's not too late to reverse this trend, each day we delay, thousands of teenagers have started to smoke. The most important task at hand is for the practitioner to become educated on the facts about smoking and youth (Figure 8.2).

According to the National Cancer Institute:

• Smoking is the chief single cause of premature mortality in this country, including about 4000 infant deaths each year.

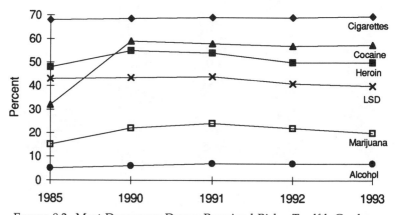

FIGURE 8.2. Most Dangerous Drugs: Perceived Risk—Twelfth-Graders

SOURCE: *National Survey Results on Drug Use from Monitoring the Future Study, 1975– 1993. Volume 1: Secondary School Students* by Lloyd D. Johnston, Patrick M. O'Malley, and Gerald G. Bachman (1994). National Institute on Drug Abuse, 5600 Fischers Lane, Rockville, MD 20857.

- Of the 3000 adolescents who begin smoking today, nearly 750 will die prematurely from a smoking-related disease.
- Smokeless tobacco use begins most often during childhood or adolescence.
- In some parts of the United States, 25%–35% of adolescent males report current use of smokeless tobacco.

Tobacco use is not simply a health problem for children but also represents a propensity for other self-destructive behavior. It's highly unlikely that young people who experiment with cigarettes will be resistant to experimentation with other destructive behaviors. For that reason, many consider tobacco a "gateway" drug to illicit substance abuse.

Many young people receive ambivalent messages about smoking and other drug use at home, so the pediatrician's office or other health care professional's office may be the only place they can be exposed to definitive information. And the younger this educational process starts, the more likely it is to have some effect.

To prevent or reduce the risk factors of tobacco use for children and adolescents, the physician must know the risk factors and be aware of children who are most vulnerable and must understand how to conduct interventions for use with children at risk and incorporate this process into each patient interaction.

If a practitioner encounters a child at risk due to smoking in the home, it is his or her responsibility to help the parents to stop or, at the very least, not to smoke around their children and expose them to secondhand smoke. The Surgeon General has said that encouraging parents to stop smoking is one of the most important obligations of a physician. Many physicians may feel uncomfortable presenting this advice and are concerned that parents may not see this as an appropriate role for the practitioner. However, it is the single most important contribution that one can make to the overall improvement of public health.[2]

How serious is tobacco use among our young people and what is the right road for professionals to follow? In 1994, the Surgeon General released the following information in her report

Preventing Tobacco Use among Young People: A Report of the Surgeon General (Figures 8.3, 8.4):

1. Nearly all first use of tobacco occurs before high school graduation; this finding suggests that if adolescents can be kept tobacco-free, most will never start using tobacco.
2. Most adolescent smokers are addicted to nicotine and report that they want to quit but are unable to do so; they experience relapse rates and withdrawal symptoms similar to those reported by adults.
3. Tobacco is often the first drug used by those young people who use alcohol, marijuana, and other drugs.
4. Adolescents with lower levels of school achievement, with fewer skills to resist pervasive influences to use tobacco, with friends who use tobacco, and with lower self-images are more likely than their peers to use tobacco.

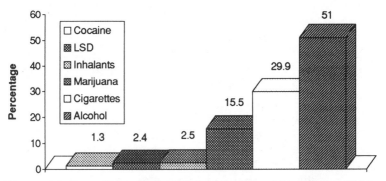

FIGURE 8.3. Drug Abuse by High School Seniors within the Past Thirty Days

SOURCE: *National Survey Results on Drug Use from Monitoring the Future Study, 1975–1993. Volume 1: Secondary School Students* by Lloyd D. Johnston, Patrick M. O'Malley, and Gerlad G. Bachman. (1994). National Institute on Drug Abuse, 5600 Fischers Lane, Rockville, MD 20857.

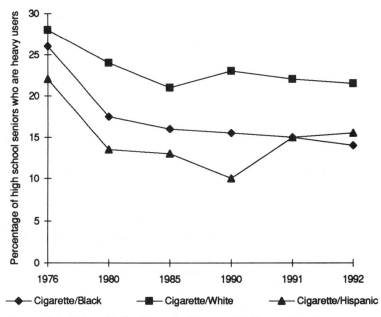

FIGURE 8.4. Heavy Daily Cigarette Use among Young People

SOURCE: U. S. National Institute on Drug Abuse. *Smoking Drinking, and Illicit Drug Use among American Secondary School Students, College Students, and Young Adults, 1975–1991. Volume I: Secondary School Students.* Rockville, MD. NIH Pub. No. 93-3480, 1992. Unpublished data from U. S. National Institute on Drug Abuse. High School Senior Survey, 1992.

5. Cigarette advertising appears to increase young people's risk of smoking by affecting their perceptions of the pervasiveness, image, and function of smoking.

6. Communitywide efforts that include tobacco tax increases, enforcement of minors' access laws, youth-oriented mass media campaigns, and school-based tobacco-use-prevention programs are successful in reducing adolescent use of tobacco.[1]

Smoking, Children, and Health Consequences

Young people suffer needlessly from tobacco use during childhood and adolescence beyond the risk factors for disease in later life. Among the findings of the U.S. Department of Health and Human Services:

- Cigarette smoking during adolescence appears to reduce the rate of lung growth and the level of maximum lung function that can be achieved.[3,4]
- Young smokers are likely to be less physically fit than young nonsmokers; fitness levels are inversely related to the duration and the intensity of smoking.
- Among young people trained as endurance runners, smoking appears to compromise physical fitness in levels of both performance and endurance since cigarette smoking reduces the oxygen-carrying capacity of the blood and increases both heart rate and basal metabolic rate—changes that counter the benefits of physical activity.[5]
- Adolescent smokers report that they are significantly more likely than their nonsmoking peers to experience shortness of breath, coughing spells, phlegm production, wheezing, and overall diminished physical health[1].
- Smoking poses a clear risk for respiratory symptoms and problems during adolescence leading to chronic conditions in adulthood, including chronic obstructive pulmonary disease (COPD).
- Adults who are lifelong smokers may have developed early inflammatory lung disorders as adolescents, which reduce lung growth, and will, as adults, have underdeveloped lung function.[6,7]
- If one or both parents of an adolescent smoke, the effects of parental smoking on early-childhood respiratory illnesses and on the growth of lung function may increase the risk of COPD. Illnesses in the lower respiratory region during childhood are a suspected risk factor for COPD.[1,8]

Heart Disease

Adolescents who smoke are at great risk for cardiovascular disease both later in life and in young adulthood. The earlier they smoke, the more likely they are to develop this disease:

- Atherosclerosis and early atherosclerotic lesions may develop earlier than usual since tobacco use has been shown to be a primary risk factor for coronary heart disease (CHD), arteriosclerotic peripheral vascular disease, and stroke.[9–12]
- According to the Surgeon General's report, the recent evidence from the PDAY Research Group shows more atherosclerosis in young smokers than in young nonsmokers. The unfavorable effects of smoking on lipid levels in children may contribute to the development of atherosclerosis in young adulthood.

Cancer

Among children, as among adults, the cancer risk from smoking is directly related to level of use and number of years,[13–15] with the risk for lung cancer varying more strongly with the duration of cigarette smoking than with the number of cigarettes smoked.[16,17]

Several reports indicate that lung cancer risk rises in direct proportion to the duration of smoking. For example, the risk at age 50 for a person who began smoking regularly at age 13 is 350% greater than that for a 50-year-old who started smoking at age 23. Other studies indicate that the younger you begin, the more you are likely to smoke and the less likely you are to be able to stop smoking.[1,9,15,18,19]

Smokeless Tobacco

As mentioned previously, smokeless tobacco use is on the rise among teens. ST use almost always begins in the early teen years, with some studies reporting "an average age of onset of 10 years."[20] High school seniors who used smokeless tobacco reported that 23% had first tried the product by the sixth grade, and 53% by the eighth grade.[1]

Smokeless tobacco (chewing tobacco and snuff) use is associated with health consequences that range from halitosis to severe health problems such as various forms of oral cancer. Use of smokeless tobacco by young people is associated with early indicators of adult health consequences, including periodontal degeneration, soft-tissue lesions, and general systemic alterations.[1]

Using smokeless tobacco is a clear risk factor for cigarette smoking. Among smokeless tobacco users, 12%–43% also smoke cigarettes. Smokeless tobacco use is also predictive of other drug use.

One study of more than 3000 male adolescents interviewed twice at nine-month intervals about their use of various psychoactive substances[21] reported that smokeless tobacco users were significantly more likely:

- To use cigarettes, marijuana, or alcohol than nonusers.
- To use these other substances by the second interview if they were not using them at the first.
- To increase their use of the substance if they also used smokeless tobacco.[1]

Addictive Behavior

Smoking leads the list of addictive behaviors for adolescents. As mentioned, if you smoke when you're young, you're likely to be a nicotine addict when you are older. But worse than that, the level of adolescent addiction is similar to that experienced by adults and can be equally difficult to stop, since withdrawal symptoms are also equal to those experienced by adults.

Tobacco as a "gateway" to other drugs of abuse *and* as a predictor of use level is well established. The 1985 NHSDA[22,23] showed that 12- to 17-year-olds who had smoked cigarettes in the past 30 days were approximately (Figure 8.5): 3 times more likely to have consumed alcohol, 8 times more likely to have smoked marijuana, and 22 times more likely to have used cocaine than those who had not smoked cigarettes.

The Surgeon General and other studies[24] report that students who, during follow-up periods, escalated from low-level use of tobacco or alcohol to heavy-level use were more likely to begin using other psychoactive substances or to increase their use of

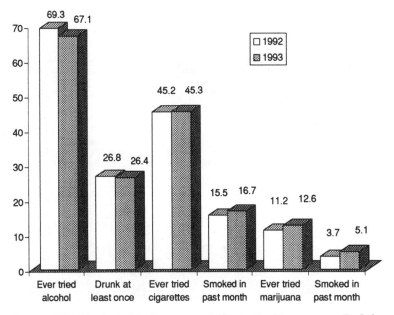

FIGURE 8.5. Alcohol, Marijuana, and Cigarette Use among Eighth-Graders, 1992–1993

SOURCE: *National Survey Results on Drug Use from Monitoring the Future Study, 1975– 1993. Volume 1: Secondary School Students* by Lloyd D. Johnston, Patrick M. O'Malley, and Gerlad G. Bachman (1994). National Institute on Drug Abuse, 5600 Fischers Lane, Rockville, MD 20857.

these substances than students who remained low-level users of tobacco or alcohol (Figure 8.6). Of all drug users surveyed by NIDA, cigarette smokers were by far the most likely to report experiencing various features of addiction.[1]

Smoking and dependency on other drugs is also well established. Among 12- to 17-year-olds who had used cigarettes, 27% were daily users and 20% felt dependent. Of those who had used alcohol, 6% were daily users and 5% felt dependent. Of those who had used marijuana, 18% were daily users and 10% felt dependent. Of those who had used cocaine, 14% were daily users and 6% felt dependent.[22,23]

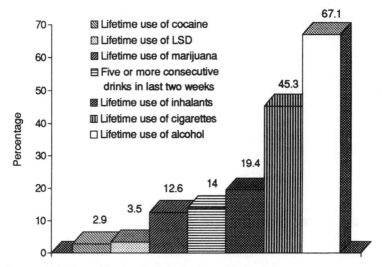

FIGURE 8.6. Drug Use by Eighth-Graders, 1993

SOURCE: *National Survey Results on Drug Use from Monitoring the Future Study, 1975–1993. Volume 1: Secondary School Students* by Lloyd D. Johnston, Patrick M. O'Malley and Gerald G. Bachman (1994). National Institute on Drug Abuse, 5600 Fischers Lane, Rockville, MD 20857.

Why Young People Smoke: Psychosocial Risk Factors

Most children experiment with cigarettes. It's almost viewed as a rite of passage from adolescence to adulthood. Yet the vast majority of teens do not become daily smokers. Why?

Recent studies indicate that there is a specific sequence of events linked to a variety of socioeconomic and psychosocial factors that most young people progress through on their way to use or nonuse[25,26] (Figure 8.7). This progression varies widely among young people and often covers a period of two to three years.[27]

In general, it can be said that adolescent tobacco use is a direct result of combined sociodemographic, environmental, behavioral, and personal factors. Teens with a lower socioeconomic status, including those adolescents living in single-parent homes, are at increased risk of initiating smoking. In fact, this group, who, in general, have lowered self-esteem and hang out with others who smoke, has reported that smoking is a status symbol. There may also be a biological drive related to nicotine's ability to enhance mood, and so on, since this group may also live under stress-related circumstances (e.g., poverty and dysfunctional families). In this case, smoking may be a "coping strategy."[28]

Since there tend to be higher levels of smoking in lower socioeconomic groups, these teens have built-in role models and fewer controls to prevent smoking or provide health risk education.[29]

The 1989 Teenage Attitudes and Practices Survey (TAPS) showed that "youths 12 through 16 years old who were current smokers were almost twice as likely to be home without a parent or other adult for 10 or more hours a week than were teens who had never smoked."

Furthermore, TAPS teens who said that they "discussed serious problems with friends rather than with a parent, other relative, or another adult" were two times more likely to be current smokers than were teens who reported discussing serious problems with their parents.[30]

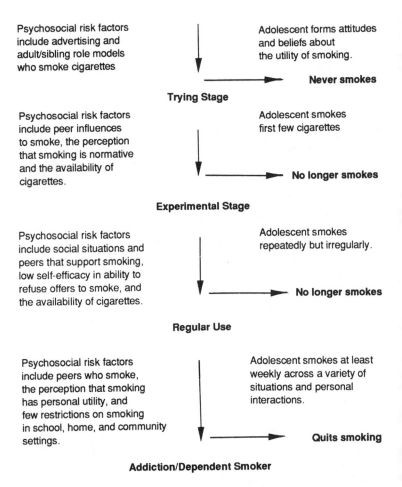

Preparatory Stage

Psychosocial risk factors include advertising and adult/sibling role models who smoke cigarettes

Adolescent forms attitudes and beliefs about the utility of smoking.

Never smokes

Trying Stage

Psychosocial risk factors include peer influences to smoke, the perception that smoking is normative and the availability of cigarettes.

Adolescent smokes first few cigarettes

No longer smokes

Experimental Stage

Psychosocial risk factors include social situations and peers that support smoking, low self-efficacy in ability to refuse offers to smoke, and the availability of cigarettes.

Adolescent smokes repeatedly but irregularly.

No longer smokes

Regular Use

Psychosocial risk factors include peers who smoke, the perception that smoking has personal utility, and few restrictions on smoking in school, home, and community settings.

Adolescent smokes at least weekly across a variety of situations and personal interactions.

Quits smoking

Addiction/Dependent Smoker

Adolescent has developed the physiological need for nicotine.

Three main factors that can predict adolescent tobacco use are parental education levels, availability, and peer pressure.[31] High school seniors who had less-educated parents were more likely to have tried a cigarette and to have adopted cigarette smoking and were less likely to have quit smoking.

Getting cigarettes is ridiculously easy for any child of any age, despite state laws prohibiting sales to minors in most states. Teens, and not unreasonably, assume that if it's available, *and legal*, it's all right to use.

The 1991 *Monitoring the Future Study* reported that 73% of 8th-graders and 88% of 10th-graders said that it would be "fairly easy" or "very easy" to get cigarettes. Others studies confirm this: a national sample of teenaged (12- to-17-year-old) smokers reported that "1.5 million of an estimated 2.6 million underage smokers buy their own cigarettes."[32] Of those who buy their own cigarettes, 84% purchase them from a small store, 50% from a large store, and 14% from a vending machine, either often or sometimes[32] (Figure 8.8).

Peer pressure for teens is often what provokes any sort of negative behavior. One study[26] suggests that smoking may primarily represent an effort to achieve social acceptance from peers and that it may particularly be an experimental "adult" activity that is shared with the peer group. Other researchers have found that smoking most often occurred in the presence of best friends.[33] In another study, among 12- to 14-year-olds,[34] those whose best

---

FIGURE 8.7. Stages of Smoking Initiation among Children and Adolescents

SOURCE: U.S. Department of Health and Human Services, *Preventing Tobacco Use among Young People: A Report of the Surgeon General*. Atlanta, GA: U.S. Department of Health and Human Services, Public Health Service, Centers for Disease Control and Prevention, National Center for Chronic Disease Prevention and Health Promotion, Office of Smoking and Health, 1994.

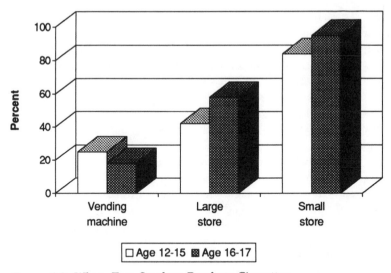

Figure 8.8. Where Teen Smokers Purchase Cigarettes

Source: U.S. Centers for Disease Control. *Morbidity and Mortality Weekly Report*, Vol. 41, No. 27, July 10, 1992.

friend smoked were four times more likely to be smokers than those whose best friend did not smoke.

Adolescents often perceive that smoking serves to make them positive role models and this is a powerful impetus to begin smoking. According to the Surgeon General's findings, "Since reports from adolescents who begin to smoke indicate that they have lower self-esteem and lower self-images than their non-smoking peers, smoking can become a self-enhancement mechanism. Not having the confidence to be able to resist peer offers of tobacco seems to be an important risk factor for initiation. Intentions to use tobacco and actual experimentation also strongly predict subsequent regular use."[1]

Adolescent smokers see cigarette use as a device for acceptance by a specific peer group, which enables them to cope with personal problems and boredom, or to be rebellious.[34] Predictors of adolescent smoking and implications for prevention. This group is rarely deterred by the initial physiological response (nausea, dizziness, etc) since the peer pressure is so strong.[36–38] The obvious conclusion is that if teenagers have more general coping skills, to help them handle the many developmental demands of adolescence, smoking will be reduced.[39]

The Surgeon General's report also points out another salient factor in teenage tobacco use: parental attitude.

> How adolescents perceive their social environment may be a stronger influence on behavior than the actual environment. Adolescents consistently overestimate the number of young people and adults who smoke. Those with the highest overestimates are more likely to become smokers, as are those who perceive that cigarettes are more easily accessible.[1]

Smokers tend to do poorly in school. Several studies[40–42] have found that those students with the highest grades smoke less than those with the lowest grades. Adolescents who had limited expectations of academic achievement also increased their smoking levels over time.[43,44]

While there is some evidence that teens who play sports or are involved in physical activities smoke a little less, these are only small measures that moderate risk.[45] In fact, even well-informed teens do not have a reduced risk,[5,42,46–48] which is shown by the fact that virtually all U.S. adolescents—smokers and nonsmokers alike—are aware of the long-term health effects of smoking. The fact is that teenagers today, as in generations past, feel that they are invulnerable, and most live for the day with very little regard to the future.[49] If for no other reason than this one—the role of the professional as a risk reduction factor in teen cigarette use is very difficult.

Some notable findings regarding young people's expectations to smoke or to abstain from smoking have emerged from the *Monitoring the Future Project.*[50]

In their senior year, respondents were asked "Do you think you will be smoking cigarettes five years from now?" Overall, about 1% said they "definitely" would be smoking in five years, 14% said they "probably" would, 27% said they probably would not, and 58% said they definitely would not. About 55% of past-month smokers and about 45% of daily smokers stated that they probably would not or definitely would not be smoking in five years. The *Monitoring the Future Project, 1985–1989*, found that as school performance among high school seniors declined from above average to below average, past-month smoking prevalence increased from 22% to 41%, and heavy smoking prevalence increased from 7% to 21%. A similar relationship was observed in the 1989 TAPS.[30]

Baiting the Hook: Tobacco Advertising and Promotional Activities

Given the data that show smoking increasing in the adolescent population, it's not surprising that the tobacco industry has cynically targeted those under 21 for their marketing efforts. If, in fact, the number of adult smokers is receding—from both cessation and fatal illness—the cigarette companies have to go somewhere to replace that loss of customers. Our children are a "revenue source" for a product that is not only illegal for them to purchase but clearly toxic.

In general, the tobacco industry uses "role model" promotional approaches, since it is banned from advertising on TV and radio. Therefore, the industry sponsors sporting events, concerts, and other activities that reach a youthful audience. In addition, tobacco companies use images that appeal to the young as glamorous and ones that they'd like to emulate. Remembering, again, that peer pressure and desire for enhanced self-image are basic drives for adolescent smoking, it's understandable how more young people respond to cigarette promotions each year.

Cigarette advertisements capitalize on the disparity between an ideal and an actual self-image and imply that smoking may close the gap. This, in turn, affects young people's perceptions of the pervasiveness, image, and function of smoking. It's these misperceptions that create psychosocial risk factors for the initiation of smoking that cigarette advertising utilizes to increase young people's risk of smoking.[1]

An excellent example is the notorious Old Joe Camel cartoon advertisements for Camel cigarettes, which are apparently far more successful at selling cigarettes to children than to adults. This finding is consistent with tobacco industry documents that indicate that a major function of tobacco advertising is to promote and maintain tobacco addiction among children.

Print advertisements are placed in magazines "specifically designed to reach young people."[51] The industry targets poster advertisements for "key youth locations/meeting places" in the proximity of theaters, record stores, video arcades, etc. The themes used in tobacco advertising that are targeted at children are the result of extensive research on children conducted by the tobacco industry to "learn everything there was to learn about how smoking begins."[52–56]

Many of the tobacco industry documents cited above provide abundant evidence that one purpose of tobacco advertising is to addict children to tobacco. In the words of one advertising consultant, "Where I worked we were trying very hard to influence kids who were 14 to start to smoke."[56,57]

Smoking and Young Women

Young women are a particularly vulnerable segment of the smoking population but, ironically, are one of the most recent targets in the tobacco industry's efforts to maintain market share.

CHAPTER 8

**Personal Advice for Adolescents Who Smoke:
The Role of the Physician**

Implications

• Generally experiment between ages 11 and 15.
• Reluctant to admit smoking when asked.
• Time perspective short-term.
• Smoke primarily for social reasons: to win peer approval, show indepen-
  dence or rebellion, look grown-up or sophisticated.

Possible Interventions

• Probe for information about smoking in a nonthreatening way.
• Avoid a disease-oriented approach that focuses on long-term consequences.
• Focus on immediate effects such as unpleasant breath, discolored teeth,
  and stained fingers.
• Discuss the acute effects of nicotine and carbon monoxide on the cardiovascular system. Relate to possible effect on performance in sports and
  other physical activities.
• Point out the fact that most adults or teens don't smoke and that patient
  shouldn't be deceived by cigarette advertising featuring young, active,
  and apparently successful young men and women as smokers.

*Source: Clinical Opportunities for Smoking Intervention: A Guide for the Busy
Physician.* U.S. Department of Health and Human Services, Public Health
Service, National Institutes of Health, 1986.

In general, women did not smoke—or at least did not smoke
publicly or in significant numbers—until after World War II, when
their smoking rose to about 25%, which was about half the number of men who smoked. Smoking among men, however, has
declined substantially from 51.9% in 1965 to 28.1% in 1991, while
women's smoking has declined by only about one-third, from
33.9% to 23.5%. It's not unlikely that soon the number of women
smoking may equal that of men.

Young women, whose self-esteem and perception of their physical appearance tend to be lower than those of boys, are a natural target for the tobacco industry, which has promoted this without shame, for example, in slogans like, "You've come a long way baby," and in sponsorship of healthful events such as the Virginia Slims Tennis Tour.[58] The tobacco industry also exploits and reinforces these vulnerabilities by linking smoking to fashion[59,60] and other images that young girls who have to live in the "real world" can never duplicate.[61]

Physicians can make a difference with young girls and should make every effort to do so, since some studies show that teenage girls do not really understand the health threats linked to smoking.[62] Unfortunately, getting teens who smoke to quit is difficult; only about 1.5% are successful.[62] Young women see physicians on average about four times a year, which offers adequate opportunity to intervene.[63]

Menstruation

There are also biological problems associated with smoking and young women. For example, there seems to be a definite, though complex, interaction between cigarette smoking and hormonal regulation. Studies of cigarette smoking and variations in female hormonal states at different times during their menstrual cycles have found that women did, in fact, smoke more frequently while menstruating. Another study found a high correlation between menstrual and withdrawal symptoms among women smokers.[64]

Pregnancy

Once it's distributed into the body, nicotine stimulates a wide variety of systems, and can travel just about anywhere. It will cross the placenta in pregnant women and enter directly into the amniotic fluid and the umbilical cord. When a pregnant woman smokes, her unborn baby is puffing away. Gestational weight at birth and birth weight tend to be lower for smokers.[65] Nicotine appears in breast milk, so a nursing mother is, in effect, giving her baby a cigarette if she smokes while nursing.

Racial Targets: Smoking Differences between Blacks and Whites

Racial divisions among smokers have been difficult to track, although it is relatively clear that Caucasians smoke more than other populations, especially African-Americans. One main difference seems to be that the white population has higher levels of nicotine dependency but lower levels of health problems associated with smoking than the African-American population.[66]

Most data show that African-Americans do not like smoking and do not accept it as proper social behavior. Studies show that they are, in general, strongly motivated to quit, but many have smoking habits that are "wake-up" habits, making cessation difficult.

Other studies report, "In general, African Americans smoke fewer cigarettes per day[67-69] and tend to begin smoking later in life than do Whites, yet their smoking-related disease mortality is higher.[70,71] Smoking fewer cigarettes also implies that African Americans should have an easier time quitting[70] but their smoking prevalence continues to exceed that of Whites,[8,9,73,74] primarily as a result of their lower success in quitting, regardless of socioeconomic status."[72] Some studies also show that blacks smoke more menthol cigarettes, which have a higher tar and nicotine content.[75-81]

Physicians and Smoking

As role models, physicians and nurses have to lead the way in presenting antismoking information to the general public, and especially to populations at high risk, such as adolescents. In doing so, many physicians and nurses have followed their own advice, and cigarette smoking has been reduced among physicians and nurses significantly over the past two decades.

As of 1991, there were, according to a study in the *Journal of the American Medical Association*,[80] 18,000 physicians, 322,000 registered nurses, and 128,000 licensed practical nurses (LPNs) who still smoked. Studies from 1974 to 1991 showed that smoking had declined from 18.8% to 3.3% among physicians, from 31.7% to 18.3% among RNs, and from 37.1% to 27.2% among LPNs.

In general, physicians have always been less likely to smoke than the rest of the population; however, smoking among nurses has always been higher than in the rest of the population. Therefore, the fact that the decline among physicians continues and that there has been a marked decline in the nursing population, indicates that education about the health effects of smoking can reduce cigarette use. In addition, these data also indicate that health care professionals are indeed beginning to see themselves as role models for those whom they treat who continue to smoke.

References

1. U.S. Department of Health and Human Services. *Preventing Tobacco Use among Young People: A Report of the Surgeon General*. Atlanta, GA: U.S. Department of Health and Human Services, Public Health Service, Centers for Disease Control and Prevention, National Center for Chronic Disease Prevention and Health Promotion, Office on Smoking and Health, 1994.
2. Glynn TJ, Manley MW. *How to Help Your Patients Stop Smoking: A National Cancer Institute Manual for Physicians*. U.S. Department of Health and Human Services, Public Health Service, National Institutes of Health, September 1992.
3. Peters JM, Ferris BG. Smoking, pulmonary function and respiratory symptoms in a college-age group. *Am Rev Resp Disease*. 1967;95(5): 774–782.
4. Beck GJ, Doyle CA, Schachter EN. A longitudinal study of respiratory health in a rural community. *Am Rev Resp Disease*. 1982;125(4):375–381.

5. Royal College of Physicians of London. *Smoking and the Young*. London: Lavenham Press, 1992.

6. Tager IB, Munoz A, Rosner B et al. Effect of cigarette smoking on the pulmonary function of children and adolescents. *Am Rev Resp Disease*. 1985;131(5):752–759.

7. Tager IB, Segal MR, Speizer FE et al. The natural history of forced expiratory volumes: Effect of cigarette smoking and respiratory symptoms. *Am Rev Resp Disease*. 1988;138(4):837–849.

8. Samet JM, Tager IB, Speizer FE. The relationship between respiratory illness in childhood and chronic air-flow obstruction in adulthood. *Am Rev Resp Disease*. 1983;127(4):508–523.

9. U.S. Department of Health and Human Services. *Reducing the Health Consequences of Smoking: 25 Years of Progress. A Report of the Surgeon General*. U.S. Department of Health and Human Services, Public Health Service, Centers for Disease Control, Center for Chronic Disease Prevention and Health Promotion, Office on Smoking and Health. DHHS Publication No. (CDC)89-8411, 1989.

10. McNamara JJ, Molot MA, Stremple JF et al. Coronary artery disease in combat casualties in Vietnam. *JAMA*. 1971;216(7):1185–1187.

11. Enos WF, Holmes RH, Beyer J. Coronary disease among United States soldiers killed in action in Korea. *JAMA*. 1986;256(20):2859–2862.

12. Strong JP. Coronary atherosclerosis in solders: A clue to the natural history of atherosclerosis in the young. *JAMA*. 1986;256(20):2863–2866.

13. Armitage P, Doll R. The age distribution of cancer and a multistage theory of carcinogenesis. *Br J Cancer*. 1954;8(1):1–11.

14. Doll R. The age distribution of cancer: Implications for models of carcinogenesis. *J Royal State Soc*. 1971;134(2):133–166.

15. Taioli E, Wynder EL. Effect of the age at which smoking begins on frequence of smoking in adulthood (letter). *N Engl J Med*. 1991; 325 (13):968–969.

16. Peto R. Epidemiology, multistage models, and short-term mutagenicity tests. In Hiatt HH, Watson JD, Winsten JA, eds., *Origins of Human Cancer, Book C, Human Risk Assessment*, Vol. 4. Cold Spring Harbor, NY: Cold Spring Harbor Laboratory, 1977.

17. Doll R, Peto R. Cigarette smoking and bronchial carcinoma: Dose and time relationships among regular smokers and lifelong non-smokers. *J Epidemiol Community Health*. 1978;32(4):303–313.

18. Escobedo LG, Marcus SE, Holtzman D et al. Sports participation, age

at smoking initiation, and the risk of smoking among US high school students. *JAMA*. 1993;269(11):1391–1395.

19. Hall EH, Terzhalmy GT. Oral manifestations of the smokeless tobacco habit. *U.S. Navy Med*. 1984;75(3):4–6.

20. U.S. Department of Health and Human Services. *Spit Tobacco and Youth*. U.S. Department of Health and Human Services, Office of Inspector General. Publication No. EI 06-92-00500, 1994.

21. Ary DV, Lichtenstein E, Severson HH. Smokeless tobacco use among male adolescents: Patterns, correlates, predictors, and the use of other drugs. *Prevent Med*. 1977;16(3):385–401.

22. U.S. Department of Health and Human Services. *The Health Consequences of Smoking: Nicotine Addiction. A Report of the Surgeon General, 1988*. U.S. Department of Health and Human Services, Public Health Service, Centers for Disease Control, Center for Health Promotion and Education, Office on Smoking and Health. DHHS Publication No. (CDC) 88-8406.

23. Henningfield JE, Clayton R, Pollin W. Involvement of tobacco in alcoholism and illicit drug use. *Br J Addiction*. 1990;85(2):279–292.

24. Baily SL. Adolescents' multisubstance use patterns: The role of heavy alcohol and cigarette use. *Am J Public Health*. 1992;82(9):1220–1224.

25. Leventhal H, Cleary PD. The smoking problem: A review of the research and theory in behavioral risk modification. *Psychol Bull*. 1980; 88(2):370–405.

26. Flay BR, D'Avernas JR, Best JA et al. Cigarette smoking: Why young people do it and ways of preventing it. In McGrath P, Firestone P, eds., *Ped Adol Behav Med*. New York: Springer-Verlag, 1983.

27. Leventhal H, Fleming R, Glynn K. A cognitive-developmental approach to smoking intervention. In Maes S, Speilbergh CD, Defares PB, Sarason IG, eds. *Topics in Health Psychology: Proceedings of the first annual expert conference in health psychology*. New York: Wiley, 1988.

28. Semmer NK, Cleary PD, Dwyer JH. Psychosocial predictors of adolescent smoking in two German cities: The Berlin-Bremen study. *Morbidity and Mortality Weekly Report*. 1987;36(4 Suppl):3S–11S.

29. Perry CL, Kelder SH, Komro KA. The social world of adolescents: Family, peers, schools, and the community. In Millstein SG, Petersen AC, Nightingale EO, eds., *Promoting the Health of Adolescents. New Directions for the Twenty-First Century*. New York: Oxford University Press, 1993.

30. Moss AJ, Allen KF, Giovino GA et al. Recent trends in adolescent

smoking, smoking-uptake correlates, and expectations about the future. *Advance Data*. U.S. Department of Health and Human Services, Public Health Service, Centers for Disease Control and Prevention, National Center for Health Statistics. No. 221. 1992.

31. Waldron I, Lye D. Relationships of teenage smoking to educational aspirations and parents' education. *J Substance Abuse*. 1990;2(2): 201–215.

32. Centers for Disease Control. Accessibility of cigarettes to youths aged 12–17 years—United States, 1989. *Morbidity and Mortality Weekly Report*. 1992;41(27):485–488.

33. Bauman KE, Foshee VA, Linzer MA et al. Effect of parental smoking classification on the association between parental and adolescent smoking. *Addict Behav*. 1990;15(5):413–422.

34. Hahn G, Charlin VL, Sussman S et al. Adolescents' first and most recent use situations of smokeless tobacco and cigarettes: Similarities and differences. *Addict Behav*. 1990;15(5):439–448.

35. Perry CL, Murray DM, Klepp K-I. Predictors of adolescent smoking and implications for prevention. *Morbidity and Mortality Weekly Report*. 1987;36(4 Suppl):41S–47S.

36. Leventhal H, Keeshan P, Baker T. Smoking prevention: Towards a process approach. *Br J Addiction*. 1991;86(5):583–587.

37. Wills TA, Shiffman S, eds. *Coping and Substance Use: A Conceptual Framework*. New York: Academic Press, 1985.

38. Castro FG, Maddahian E, Newcomb MD et al. A multivariate model of the determinants of cigarette smoking among adolescents. *J Health Soc Behav*. 1987;28(3):273–289.

39. Franzkowiak P. Risk-taking and adolescent development: The functions of smoking and alcohol consumption in adolescence and its consequences for prevention. *Health Promotion*. 1987;2(1):51–61.

40. Borland BL, Rudolph JP. Relative effects of low socioeconomic status, parental smoking and poor scholastic performance on smoking among high school students. *Soc Sci Med*. 1975;9(1):27–30.

41. Brunswick AF, Messeri PA. Origins of cigarette smoking in academic achievement, stress and social expectations: Does gender make a difference? *J Early Adol*. 1984;4(4):353–370.

42. Sussman S, Dent CW, Flay BR et al. Psychosocial predictors of cigarette smoking onset by white, black, Hispanic, and Asian adolescents in Southern California. *Morbidity and Mortality Weekly Report*. 1987; 36(4 Suppl):11S–17S.

43. Gerber RW, Newman IM. Predicting future smoking of adolescent experimental smokers. *J Youth Adol.* 1989;18(2):191–201.
44. Chassin L, Presson CC, Sherman SJ et al. Four pathways to young-adult smoking status: Adolescent social-psychological antecedents in a Midwestern community sample. *Health Psychol.* 1991;10(6): 409–418.
45. Rantakallio P. Family background to and personal characteristics underlying teenage smoking. *Scand J Social Med.* 1983;11(1):17–22.
46. Collins LM, Sussman S, Rauch JM et al. Psychosocial predictors of young adolescent cigarette smoking: A sixteen-month three-wave longitudinal study. *J Appl Soc Psychol.* 1987;17(6):554–573.
47. Krohn MD, Naughton MJ, Lauer RM. Adolescent cigarette use: The relationship between attitudes and behavior. *Morbidity and Mortality Weekly Report.* 1987;36(4 Suppl):25S–35S.
48. Conrad KM, Flay BR, Hill D. Why children start smoking cigarettes: Predictors of onset. *Br J Addiction.* 1992;87(12):1711–1724.
49. Gerber RW, Newman IM. Predicting future smoking of adolescent experimental smokers. *J Youth Adol.* 1989;18(2):191–201.
50. Johnson LD, O'Malley RM, Bachman JG. *Smoking, Drinking and Illicit Drug Use Among American Secondary School Students, College Students, and Young Adults, 1975-1991*, Vol. 1. U.S. Department of Health and Human Services, Public Health Service, National Institutes of Health, National Institute on Drug Abuse. Bethesda (MD): NIH Publication No. 93-3480, 1992.
51. RJR-MacDonald Document 286. P1980-1(*RJR-MacDonald Inc. & Imperial Tobacco v. the Attorney General of Canada*).
52. *Report for Imperial Tobacco Ltd.* Montreal, Quebec: Kwechansky Marketing Research Inc: 1977. Project 16 (*RJR-MacDonald Inc. & Imperial Tobacco v. the Attorney General*).
53. *Report for Imperial Tobacco Ltd.* Kwechansky Marketing Research Inc, 1982. Project PLUS/MINUS (*RJR-MacDonald Inc. & Imperial Tobacco v. the Attorney General of Canada*).
54. *Youth 1987.* The Creative Research Group Ltd: 1987. Prepared for RJR-MacDonald (*RJR-MacDonald Inc. & Imperial Tobacco v. the Attorney General of Canada*).
55. *Report to RJR-MacDonald Inc: Third Family Qualitative Concept Test.* Toronto, Ontario: Cogemic Marketing, 1981 (*RJR-MacDonald Inc. & Imperial Tobacco v. the Attorney General of Canada*).
56. *Report to Congress Pursuant to the Cigarette Smoking Act 1978: An Action*

Oriented Research Program for Discovering and Creating the Best Possible Image for Viceroy Cigarettes. Ted Bates Advertising. Washington, DC: Federal Trade Commission. Document AD11345, 1975.

57. DiFranza JR, Richards JW, Paulman PM. RJR Nabisco's cartoon camel promotes Camel cigarettes to children. *JAMA.* 1991;266(22):3149–3153.

58. Minigawa K, While D, Charlton A. Smoking and self-perception in secondary school students. *Tobacco Control.* 1993;2:215–221.

59. Ernster VL. Mixed messages for women: a social history of cigarette smoking and advertising. *NY State J Med.* 1985;85:335–340.

60. Simpson D. Smoking and fashion. *Tobacco Control.* 1993;2:244–245.

61. Bohner K. Smoke and mirrors. *Forbes.* November 8, 1993:316.

62. Preliminary Data: National Health Interview Survey on Teenage Attitudes and Practices (TAPS II). National Center for Health Statistics; Hyattsville MD, 1993.

63. Smoking and young women: The physician's role in stopping an equal opportunity killer. *JAMA.* 1994;271(8):629–630.

64. Pomerleau CS, Garcia AW, Pomerleau OF et al. The effects of menstrual phase and nicotine abstinence on nicotine intake and on biochemical and subjective measures in women smokers: A preliminary report. *Psychoneuroendocrinology.* 1992;17(6):627–638.

65. Kleiman MA. *Against Excess.* New York: Basic Books, 1992.

66. Andreski P, Breslau N. Smoking and nicotine dependence in young adults: Differences between blacks and whites. *Drug and Alcohol Dependence.* 1993;32:119–125.

67. *Prevention '89/90—Federal Programs and Progress.* U.S. Department of Health and Human Services. Washington, DC, 1990.

68. Garfinkel L. Cigarette smoking and coronary heart disease in blacks: Comparison to whites in a prospective study. *Am Heart J.* 1984; 108:802–807.

69. Centers for Disease Control. Cigarette smoking among adults—United States, 1988. *MMWR.* 1991;40:757–759, 765.

70. Escobedo LG, Anda RF, Smith PF et al. Sociodemographic characteristics of cigarette smoking initiation in the United States: Implications for smoking prevention policy. *JAMA.* 1990;264:1550–1555.

71. Centers for Disease Control. Differences in the age of smoking initiation between blacks and whites—United States, 1991. *MMWR.* 1991; 40:754–757.

72. McWorter WP, Boyd GM, Mattson ME. Predictors of quitting smoking: the NHANES I follow-up experience. *J Clin Epidemiol.* 1990; 43:1399–1405.

73. Fiore MC, Novotny TE, Pierce JP et al. Trends in cigarette smoking in the United States—The changing influence of gender and race. *JAMA*. 1989;261:499–55.
74. Novotny TE, Warner KE, Kendrick JS et al. Smoking by blacks and whites: Socioeconomic and demographic differences. *Am J Public Health*. 1988;78:1187–1189.
75. Cummings MK, Giovino G. Mendicine AJ et al. Cigarette advertising and black-white differences in brand preference. *Public Health Rep*. 1987;102:698–701.
76. Davis RM, Healy P, Hawk SA. Information on tar and nicotine yields on cigarette packages. *Am J Public Health*. 1990;80:551–553.
77. Hebert JR, Kabat GC. Menthol cigarettes and esophageal cancer (letter). *Am J Public Health*. 1988;78:986–987.
78. Kabat GC, Morabia A, Wynder EL. Comparisons of smoking habits of blacks and whites in a case-control study. *Am J Public Health*. 1991;81: 1483–1486.
79. Orleans CT, Schoenback VJ, Salmon MA et al. A survey of smoking and quitting patterns among black Americans. *Am J Public Health*. 1989;79:176–181.
80. Sidney S, Tekawa I, Friedman GD. Mentholated cigarette use among multiphasic examinees, 1979–1986. *Am J Public Health*. 1989;79:1415–1416.
81. Royce JM, Hymowitz N, Corbett K et al. Smoking cessation factors among African Americans and whites. *Am J Public Health*. 1993;83(2): 220–226.
82. Nelson DE, Giovano GA, Emont SL et al. Cigarette smoking trends among physicians and nurses. *JAMA*. 1994;271(16):1273–1775.

9

Prevention and Education

Over the past decade, those of us involved in reducing substance abuse (e.g., marijuana, cocaine, opiates), have focused our efforts on creating a drug-free generation. The idea, of course, is that once we can break the cycle of use, the following generations will also follow the example of their now drug-free parents. This is an even more crucial goal for those involved in trying to prevent cigarette smoking. As is made clear in the preceding chapters, nicotine addiction begins when users are adolescents and threatens their health over decades. In order to break this cycle, physicians and other health care professionals will have to battle constantly against a clever and well-financed enemy.

Consider, for example, what the practitioner today has to overcome. A prominent cigarette manufacturer targets readers of youth-oriented publications, such as *Rolling Stone Magazine*, with very expensive, full-color inserts advertising the availability of premium products from the cigarette manufacturer's "country store." Items such as jean jackets, sporting equipment, and other "hip gear" are available, not by purchase, but only by the accumulation of "miles." These miles, just like frequent-flier miles, have to be earned. But in this case, the miles are accumulated not through travel, but specifically through the number of cigarettes smoked. If you wish to get the jean jacket, you have to provide proof of smoking 160 packs of cigarettes. How can physicians and others interested in stopping smoking overcome such cynical—and clearly effective—marketing of a product that is lethal.

It is not an easy job. According to the Robert Wood Johnson Foundation,[1] over the past several decades, numerous regulations to control the sale, marketing and use of tobacco products have been initiated:

- Cigarette advertising on television and radio was discontinued more than two decades ago.
- Several states restrict cigarette advertising on state or local government property, including buses, transit stations and sports facilities.
- In almost every state the minimum age to buy cigarettes is 18
- Smoking bans—partial or total restrictions on public smoking—have been adopted by 46 states, the District of Columbia, and about 500 municipalities. The states with few or no restrictions are concentrated in the South, and those with the most extensive restrictions are in the eastern and north-central states.

The result has been that the vast majority of Americans want cigarette smoking banned in all public places, from hotels to restaurants to the workplace, and there is considerable support for the use of increased cigarette taxes to support antidrug and health care programs.[1]

Fortunately, programs that previously focused only on alcohol and illegal drugs are now shifting to include tobacco and smoking programs that are aimed at adolescents and children. However, this is a fight that must be waged on many fronts.

For example, the most dramatic change in attitudes toward smoking has probably taken place at the work site. It is far more common to see small groups of employees standing outside, even in bitter cold weather, on a smoke break than it is to see the majority of people sitting at their desks, chain smoking as they did in the past. About two-thirds of American companies and most state and federal agencies now provide stop-smoking programs and even incentives for employees who successfully quit. Companies strapped by rising health care costs have been quick to admit that cigarette smoking is as dangerous to their employees as other substances of abuse.[1]

Even though most of us believe that simply banning cigarettes is the quick and direct solution to this problem, it is unlikely that this will occur. The reality is that tobacco and alcohol use are part of our cultural heritage. In addition, while it's relatively clear that the health effects of tobacco and nicotine are negative, they, too, are part of a complex problem. Simply banning cigarettes would not, for example, rid the population of pulmonary or cardiovascular disease, so the only way to solve the problems caused by tobacco use is to create programs that focus on all aspects of prevention, including both legal and illegal drugs, along with other good health programs.

As suggested by Wandersman and Goodman, "Community-wide problems require community-wide solutions. The strategies for these solutions must involve collaboration among community organizations and institutions as well as a renewed faith in citizen participation. Coalitions of community agencies, institutions and concerned citizens represent one promising strategy for designing interventions that operate at multiple levels of the social ecology."[2]

Physicians and other health care professionals can become the leaders in the development of these community-wide coalitions that are, in effect, the best form of treatment for nicotine addiction. Professionals must be involved in every aspect of this problem, from creating their own office-based program, as described in this book, to assisting in the development of grant proposals to help fund these projects.

Above all, we must not forget that our most important goal is to prevent smoking in the population most at risk, our children. As advocated by the U.S. Department of Health, we must make sure that tobacco education programs are in every school system; that educators lead the way by banning smoking around and near schools; that we write to congressional and regulatory bodies to demand further restrictions on tobacco advertising and promotional activities; and, of course, that we make ourselves available to groups that wish to have expert advice (Table 9.1).

These programs can work. According to the U.S. Surgeon General:

> Numerous research studies over the past 15 years suggest that organized interventions can help prevent the onset of smoking and smokeless tobacco use. School-based smoking-prevention programs, based on a model of identifying social influences on smoking and providing skills to resist those influences, have demonstrated consistent and significant reductions in adolescent smoking prevalence; these program effects have lasted one to three years. The effectiveness of these school-based programs appears to be enhanced and sustained at least until high school graduation, by adding coordinated communitywide programs that involve parents, youth-oriented mass media and counter advertising, community organizations, or other elements of adolescents' social environments.[3]

If the laws preventing sale of cigarettes to minors are enforced, and if the cost of cigarettes is put out of the reach of our young people, we can make a difference and, perhaps, achieve the goal of a "smoke-free" generation.

Education Is the Best Measure of Prevention

It is generally believed by clinicians that education is prevention. For example, when asked about their prevention activities, many physicians and health providers describe lectures and patient education sessions. Over the past decade, a science of prevention has emerged, thanks to objective measures and scientific methodologies applied to prevention and control interventions. By studying a group of fifth- or sixth-grade students over a decade, scientists have a much better idea of what is the natural history of nicotine dependence or smoking initiation and what can be done to prevent it in the first place. Primary prevention can be effective (Table 9.2).

Recent work by groups in Kansas City, New York City, Los Angeles, and elsewhere suggest that reductions of 50% are possible with a well-conceived, vigorous program. Most of these programs (facilitated by a classroom teacher or Drug Abuse Resistance Education [DARE] officer) do not teach the facts about a particular drug; rather, they teach children the skills needed to resist and reduce the effects of social pressure.

Physicians have an important role to play as well. They are well-respected authorities on disease and treatment, but their influence is limited by the fact that they see a patient for a short time and at infrequent intervals, and their role at such times is often authoritarian. The physician in many communities is the expert in prevention, disease, addiction, and public health. As the expert, the physician needs to be familiar with certain facts of life in the science of prevention.

First, disseminating information is not prevention. It is now clear that you can teach a child or an adult about the effects of cigarette smoking on health, prove that you taught them by virtue of a posttest, and not have any effect whatsoever on smoking rates. Second, changing attitudes about cigarettes or drugs may have slightly better effects on smoking behavior—especially in those who have not started—but attitude change appears to be independent of behavior change. Third, of all of the nonfamily/nongenetic or host factors impacting on cigarette use, a child's group of friends and associates and their cigarette or drug use appear to be quite important as a determinant. Students will generally overestimate the number of the people their age who smoke, drink, or use this or that drug.

This overestimation creates the widespread belief that their

TABLE 9.1. Overview of Major Preventive Approaches

Approach	Focus	Methods
Information dissemination	Increase knowledge of drugs and the consequences of use; promote antidrug use attitudes	Didactic instruction, discussion, audio/video presentations, displays of substances, posters, pamphlets, school assembly programs
Affective education	Increase self-esteem, responsible decision making, interpersonal growth; generally includes little or no information about drugs	Didactic instruction, discussion, experiential activities, group problem-solving exercises
Alternatives	Increase self-esteem, self-reliance; provide variable alternatives to drug use; reduce boredom and sense of alienation	Organization of youth centers, recreational activities; participation in community service projects; vocational training
Resistance skills	Increase awareness of social influence to smoke, drink, or use drugs; develop skills for resisting substance use influences; increase knowledge of immediate negative consequences; establish non-substance-use norms	Class discussion; resistance skills training; behavioral rehearsal; extended practice via behavioral "homework"; use of same-age or older peer leaders

TABLE 9.1. (*Continued*)

Approach	Focus	Methods
Personal and social skills training	Increase decision making, personal behavior change, anxiety reduction, communication, social, and assertive skills; application of generic skills to resist substance use influences	Class discussion; cognitive-behavioral skills training (instruction, demonstration, practice, feedback, reinforcement)

Source: G. J. Botvin and E. M. Botvin. "School-Based and Community-Based Prevention Approaches" In J. H. Lowinstein, P. Ruiz, and R. B. Millman, eds., *Substance Abuse: Comprehensive Textbook*. Baltimore: Williams & Wilkins, 1992.

behavior is normal and OK. If a child's best friend smokes cigarettes or uses drugs, then the peer pressure will chronically weigh on that child to try, to use, to fit in. Recognizing peer pressure or social influence involves understanding that all peer environments are different within the same school and even in the same family in the same school. Prevention, in the context of a multiweek course at school with periodic "boosters," appears to work by reducing the impact of social influence, providing positive resistance skills, and supporting the development of "no-saying" protective factors.

Physicians need to understand the power of prevention activities in reducing cigarette smoking, as well as the differences between fact training or attitude training and prevention, and to provide expert advice to the school, police or other providers on the value of prevention efforts and methodology. Trained as a scientist, the physician is also a well-trained expert on the need for baseline use and longitudinal follow-up data to evaluate the program which the school has implemented.

This is a different role for the physician from the traditional

TABLE 9.2. Studies Testing Informational Approaches

Investigator(s)	Subjects	Intervention approach	Evaluation design	Results
Degnan (1972)	9th-grade students	10 weeks; information-based	Pre- and posttest	No significant attitude changes
Richardson et al. (1972)	5th-grade students	10 hours; information-based (film strips, speakers, discussion)	Pre- and posttest	No significant attitude changes
Weir (1968)	High school students	Not clearly described	Repeated administration of questionnaire	Significant attitude changes
Friedman (1973)	7th- and 8th-grade students	One class period/week for 14 weeks; illustrations of drug-related situations and decisions	Pre- and posttest questionnaires	Significant attitude changes

O'Rourke and Barr (1974)	High school students	6-month course using New York State curriculum guide	Posttest only	Significant attitude changes for males only
Mason (1973)	8th- and 12th-grade students	Information-based; length not reported	Pre- and posttest	Increased knowledge: increased drug curiosity and tendency toward increased usage
Rosenblitt and Nagey (1973)	7th-grade students	Six 45-min. sessions; information-based, presented as reasons for use and nonuse	Pre- and posttest; no control group	Increased knowledge; trend toward increased usage of alcohol and tobacco
Stenmark et al. (1977)	College undergraduates and pharmacy students	2 to 4 years college-level pharmacy course work	Pre- and posttest	Pharmacy students had more knowledge about and more liberal attitudes toward drugs

Source: G. J. Botvin and E. M. Botvin. "School-Based and Community-Based Prevention Approaches" In J. H. Lowinstein, P. Ruiz, and R. B. Millman, eds., *Substance Abuse: Comprehensive Text Book.* Baltimore: Williams & Wilkins, 1992.

role of assessing cigarette or drug use, detailing the history, evaluating for consequences, and starting a discontinuation program.

There are many different approaches to prevention of and education about tobacco abuse. However, it cannot be forgotten that the problem of smoking among young people is a substance abuse problem, not unlike any other substance abuse problem. According to Gilbert and Elizabeth Botvin,[4] the best programs are school- and community-based. Here are their conclusions:

> A number of substance abuse prevention approaches have been developed and tested over the years. The most common approaches to tobacco, alcohol, and drug abuse prevention are those that focus on providing factual information about the adverse consequences of using these substances, with some approaches including a mix of scare tactics and moral messages. Other commonly used approaches to substance abuse prevention have utilized affective education and alternative approaches. The existing evaluation literature shows rather conclusively that these are not effective prevention strategies when the standard of effectiveness concerns the ability to influence substance use behavior.
>
> The only prevention approaches that have been demonstrated to effectively impact on substance use behavior are those that teach junior high school students social resistance skills either alone or in combination with approaches designed to enhance general personal competence by teaching an array of personal and social life skills. Both approaches emphasize skills training and reemphasize the provision of information concerning the adverse health consequences of substance use. These approaches utilize well-tested behavioral intervention techniques to facilitate the acquisition of skills for resisting social influences to engage in substance use.
>
> Recognizing the critical importance of the early adolescent years, these preventive interventions have generally been implemented with middle and junior high school students. Despite generally impressive prevention effects, it is

clear that, without booster sessions, these effects decay over time, thus arguing for ongoing prevention activities throughout early adolescent years and perhaps until the end of high school.

Although there has been considerable activity in the form of both the parents' movement and mass media campaigns, there is little evidence to indicate that such approaches are effective when used alone. However, community-based substance abuse prevention approaches based on principles derived from the most effective school-based prevention programs and successful community-based cardiovascular disease prevention studies appear to offer considerable promise.

Over the past decade, there have been a number of significant developments in the field of substance abuse prevention. Yet, despite the promise offered by these approaches, future research is needed to further refine current prevention models and to develop new ones. Given the urgency and importance of dealing with the problem of substance abuse, it seems prudent to proceed on two simultaneous tracks: one involving further prevention research and the other involving the dissemination of the most promising existing prevention approaches. This is particularly important in view of the fact that the most widely utilized prevention approaches continue to be those that have already been found either to be ineffective or to lack any scientifically defensible evidence of their efficacy.

The problem of substance abuse is still very prevalent. However, for the first time in the history of its prevention, evidence now exists from a number of rigorously designed evaluation studies that specific school-based and community-based prevention models are effective. It is now incumbent upon health care professionals, educators, community leaders, and policy makers to move expeditiously toward wide dissemination and utilization of these approaches. It is equally important for private and governmental agencies to provide adequate funding for the important research necessary to further refine existing prevention models and to increase our understanding of the causes of substance abuse.

How to Help Your Patients Stop Smoking:
More Ideas from the National Cancer Institute
Manual for Physicians

School Programs to Prevent Smoking

Most schools have a health education curriculum and, increasingly, tobacco use prevention is being incorporated into that course work. There is evidence that school programs to prevent smoking do have positive effects on delaying the onset of smoking.

As role models in the community, physicians have many opportunities to encourage schools to implement tobacco use prevention programs and to participate in developing and teaching such programs. Medical groups and physicians can act as advocates for such programs and can work closely with health, physical education, and science teachers and trainers in the selection of a curriculum.

Fortunately it is not necessary for a health-related curriculum to focus only on smoking to succeed. Smoking can be part of a broader health curriculum as long as a minimum of five classroom sessions in each of two years are devoted to the topic. A one-year program is not enough. Booster sessions in subsequent years appear essential for sustained program effects.

Ideally, tobacco use prevention programs should be offered in all grades, including elementary school. Where this approach is not feasible, program efforts should begin at the time smoking most often begins: in Grades 6 or 7, whichever is the first year after elementary school. Programs should continue at least through Grade 9. The sixth- to ninth-grade period is when young people seem to be most vulnerable to taking up smoking. It is also the opportunity to provide information about smoking to those who may drop out of school after the ninth grade.

At a minimum, tobacco use prevention programs should include the following:

1. Information about the social influences on tobacco use—especially peer, parent, and media influences.

   2. Information about tobacco's short-term effects on the body.

   3. Training in refusal skills, including modeling and practice of resistance skills.

Parental support is important for the effectiveness of school-based tobacco use prevention programs. However, active parental participation is not essential.

Teachers should be trained thoroughly to present a prevention curriculum. Ideally, training should last a full day and include opportunities to role-play and interact with student assistants. The most effective programs are led by teachers with students assisting in the delivery. Successful programs delay the onset of smoking among young participants. By simply delaying smoking onset, school programs: (1) reduce the chance that these youth, even if they become smokers, will eventually develop lung cancer and other smoking-related disease; (2) reduce the possibility that they will become regular smokers as adults; and (3) make it easier for those who do start smoking to stop.

School Tobacco Use Policies

Physicians can also play an important role in supporting smoke-free environments in schools and in advocating a total ban on tobacco use on school grounds. As community leaders, doctors often have opportunities to influence local school boards and governing bodies in the policy decisions that can affect cigarette smoking among youth and adults.

Tobacco Advertising Targeted to Youth

Physicians can work in their communities to oppose advertising of all tobacco products, especially those advertisements that target young people. At times, cigarette advertisements attempt to allay anxieties about the hazards of smoking. Some advertisements falsely associate smoking with good health, athletic vigor, and social and professional success. Usually the cigarette is portrayed as an integral part of youth, happiness, attractiveness, personal success, and a vigorous lifestyle.

The success of advertising campaigns is evident in the fact that youth greatly overestimate the prevalence of smoking among peers and adults, including their teachers. These perceptions about societal norms lead to acceptance of tobacco use. Physicians can help correct these beliefs by providing children and adolescents with a more accurate picture of cigarette use.

Sale of Tobacco to Minors

Virtually anyone, of any age can easily purchase cigarettes over the counter and from vending machines. Physicians can promote and assist community organizations in developing merchant education programs to reduce illegal cigarette sales to minors in all types of stores. Communities can also mandate the removal of unsupervised vending machines as an effective way to prevent minors from purchasing cigarettes.

Physicians can effectively advocate laws that eliminate minors' access to tobacco by providing expert testimony on the problems of tobacco use in children and adolescents. Following is a list of organizations, provided by the National Cancer Institute, which are working to decrease tobacco use among young people. For support in these efforts, physicians should contact one or more of these groups.

AMERICAN CANCER SOCIETY
1599 Clifton Road, NE
Atlanta, GA 30329
404-320-3333

AMERICAN HEART ASSOCIATION
7320 Greenville Avenue
Dallas, TX 75231
214-750-5300

AMERICAN LUNG ASSOCIATION
1740 Broadway
New York, NY 10019
212-315-8700

DOCTORS OUGHT TO CARE (DOC)
HH-101
Medical College of Georgia
Augusta, GA 30912

References

1. *Substance Abuse: The Nation's Number One Health Problem. Key Indicators for Policy*. Princeton, NJ: The Robert Wood Johnson Foundation, 1993.
2. Wandersman A, Goodman R. Comprehensive community coalitions to prevent alcohol, tobacco and other drug abuse. In Miller N., ed., *Principles of Addiction Medicine*. ASAM Review Course Syllabus. American Society of Addiction Medicine, 1994.
3. U.S. Department of Health and Human Services. *Preventing Tobacco use among Young People: A Report of the Surgeon General*. Atlanta, GA: U.S. Department of Health and Human Services, Public Health Service, Centers for Disease Control and Prevention, National Center for Chronic Disease Prevention and Health Promotion, Office on Smoking and Health, 1994.
4. Botvin GJ, Botvin EM. School-based and community-based prevention approaches. In Lowenstein JH, Ruiz P, Millman RB, eds., *Substance Abuse: Comprehensive Textbook*. Baltimore: Williams & Wilkins, 1992.

Additional Source

Glynn TJ, Manley MW. *How to Help Your Patients Stop Smoking: A National Cancer Institute Manual for Physicians*. U.S. Department of Health and Human Services, Public Health Service, National Institutes of Health, 1992.

Index

Italics denote figures; t denotes tables.